Praise for the Innovative Leaders Workbook to Implementing Analytics Programs

Maureen and James have provided invaluable information to help you successfully implement an analytics or Big Data initiative. Their pragmatic method is direct and adaptable to any organization or program. The examples are thought provoking and will help you improve your innovative leadership abilities.

Peter Mooiweer, IBM, Partner

▰▰▰▰▰▰▰

This workbook offers leaders a pragmatic approach and the necessary tools to lead a successful analytics implementation. At the same time, readers and leaders are introduced to unique techniques to refine their leadership skills in order to effectively lead the changes they are making to their organizations. The combination of leadership building and leading analytics implementation make this a must-use tool when implementing an analytics program.

Angelo Mazzocco, Chief Information Officer at COPCP

▰▰▰▰▰▰▰

This workbook provides a great approach from two seasoned leaders. Maureen and James have combined their insights to give you a step-by-step approach to developing your leadership team and delivering results. It is easy to apply to a variety of organizations and challenges.

Phil Smith, CIO, Wasserstrom, Inc.

▰▰▰▰▰▰▰

The Innovative Leadership Workbook for Implementing Analytics Programs provides a great synthesis of proven effective leadership and change management theories and practices, and applies them to make specific strategic change possible within technical cultures and environments. This effectively melds soft and hard skills into a planned and deliberate approach that will make a difference when implementing technical change. Nicely done.

Scott Caine, CEO, GroundWork group

▰▰▰▰▰▰▰

This workbook is an absolute must for every executive that wants to create an analytics program in his or her company. By following the activities, guidelines, and suggestions, such a program is more likely to succeed, and generate a positive ROI sooner.

Michael A. Levin, Ph.D., Associate Professor, Marketing, Otterbein University, Department of Business, Accounting, and Economics

Innovative Leadership Workbook for Implementing Analytics Programs is very practical book on how to use transformational leadership to stay ahead in innovation while implementing large scale change projects.

Leadership is the foundation for effective transformation, Maureen and James in this workbook provide a framework, processes and guidance to successfully implement innovation change programs efficiently and effectively. This framework, tools and processes are based on their work with hundreds of companies over the last 5 years.

If you're looking for a practical guide book supported by many examples, clear and easy to follow that will support you to succeed in the area of innovative leadership, the workbook by Maureen and James is a must read.

Alan Crookes, Head of Financial Services, Asia Pacific Region, BMW Group

■■■■■■■

Regardless of your industry, James and Maureen have provided a thorough workbook focused on your success. The process is comprehensive and the examples easily applied to your situation.

James Paat, CEO, InXite Health Systems

■■■■■■■

The complexity of analytics implementation impacts every area of an organization and requires a solid understanding of the organization as a living system. This workbook melds the art and science required to lead analytics programs in such complex environment and delivery significant strategic advantage. It is a must read!

Stacey Clark, Senior Manager, Emerging Technologies and Innovation, Walmart Inc.

■■■■■■■

Whether this is your first or fifth analytics transformation, the framework established in this workbook can guide you to greater success. Beyond leading the actual initiative, this book will help develop your leadership abilities.

Shane Gianino, CEO, Qstride, Inc.

INNOVATIVE
LEADERS WORKBOOK
TO IMPLEMENTING
ANALYTICS PROGRAMS

Field-Tested Processes and Templates for Innovating Leadership
and Implementing Data and Analytics Programs

MAUREEN METCALF   JAMES BRENZA

FORWARD BY THORNTON A. MAY, *FUTURIST*

First Published by
Integral Publishers
1418 N. Jefferson Ave.
Tucson, AZ 85712

Published in the United States with printing and
distribution in the United Kingdom, Australia, and
the European Union.

ISBN: 978-0-9904419-2-2

First Printing September 2014

Cover Design, Graphics and Layout by
Creative Spot - www.creativespot.com

Acknowledgments

Contributing authors who helped to make this book a reality: Kathleen Bergen, Kathryn Burgess, Mike Morrow-Fox, Belinda Gore, Ph.D., and Mark Palmer.

This book represents the synthesis of twenty-five years of research, work experience, and consulting for each of the primary authors. It integrates best practices from consulting firms, colleagues, nonprofits, and clients. We would first like to acknowledge our former employers for providing practical opportunities to learn and build strong skills in leadership, analytics, consulting, organizational change, large-scale systems change, and strategic thinking, among many others. It was this solid foundation that allowed us to create this methodology.

As a theoretical foundation, we worked with or studied the work of many thought leaders in the fields of leadership development, developmental psychology, integral theory, and others. The theoretical giants on whose hard work we built the Innovative Leadership and Organizational Transformation models include Terri O'Fallon, Ph.D., Susanne Cook-Greuter, Ph.D., Hilke Richmer, Ph.D., Roxanne Howe-Murphy, Ed.D., Ken Wilber. These leaders shared not only their theories, but ongoing guidance and encouragement, helping to create a solid framework that is comprehensive and theoretically grounded.

Friends and colleagues who served as constant cheerleaders and readers, made suggestions, listened to stories and dreams about the book, and helped make it come to fruition; the teachers, trainers, and mentors who taught how to lead—and when to follow.

Family who provided continual support and encouragement as well as inspiring us to be thoughtful, dedicated to work, and to contribute to the world in a meaningful way.

Publisher and friend, Russ Volckmann, Ph.D.

Graphic design and layout firm Creative Spot, editorial team who checked and edited at every turn: Mary Wood, Eric Philippou, and Rachel Bruce as well as other editors, reviewers, endorsers, thought partners, and countless others who spent untold hours making this workbook possible.

Table of Contents

FOREWORD

As a modern and ethical futurist, I do not generate predictions; (That is the purview of substance abusing Delphic priestesses and many of my not-to-be-mentioned-by-name-obsessed-to-generate-headlines colleagues in the futures industry.) I craft perspective. One does not need to be a card-carrying futurist to recognize that the master narrative pulsing from three screens (computer, smartphone, and TV) and traditional media alike is the overwhelmingly accepted belief that:

We are living in a transformative time.

This is true. We are living in a transformative time. What many don't realize is that we have been living in a transformative time for the past 600 years. Change is inevitable and has occurred throughout the ages.

Change is accelerating (relative to data growth and computing capacity to harness it), and you need to take action at the inflection points. Former Intel Chairman Andy Grove said, that an inflection point "occurs where the old strategic picture dissolves and gives way to the new." This seems to be happening with disconcerting regularity. Every day, contemporary executives confront a series of inflection points—situations in which current wisdom is no longer adequate or appropriate for the task at hand. Francois Hollande became the president of France on the promise of being "Mr. Normal." His record-setting low popularity suggests that, *"at least in France, there is no place for normal,"* as *The New York Times* put it. That may be true everywhere. Here's the thing: Great leaders are able to imagine, and hence control, what is on the other side of the inflection point.

As we move forward from this inflection point, un-augmented human cognition (the *old know*) is not sufficient. In every vertical market and just about every field of human endeavor, the magical carbon-chemo-electro process known as thinking and the heretofore unaudited mysterious arts of decision making have to be linked with the tools, processes, and practices of business analytics. The mantra of the New Know age is to expeditiously understand and then efficaciously act.

Organizations must look for new methods to harness this opportunity. They must truly transform their thinking to embrace more responsive strategies, align teams more dynamically, and creatively solve resource shortages. Big data paired with analytics is one solution to harness these opportunities.

What is Big Data?

"Every day, we create 2.5 quintillion bytes of data—so much that 90% of the data in the world today has been created in the last two years alone. This data comes from everywhere: sensors used to gather climate information, posts to social media sites, digital pictures and videos, purchase transaction records, and cell phone GPS signals to name a few. This data is big data.

Big data spans three dimensions: Volume, Velocity and Variety.

Volume: Enterprises are awash with ever-growing data of all types, easily amassing terabytes—even petabytes—of information.

- Turn 12 terabytes of Tweets created each day into improved product sentiment analysis

- Convert 350 billion annual meter readings to better predict power consumption

Velocity: Sometimes 2 minutes is too late. For time-sensitive processes such as catching fraud, big data must be used as it streams into your enterprise in order to maximize its value.

- Scrutinize 5 million trade events created each day to identify potential fraud

- Analyze 500 million daily call detail records in real-time to predict customer churn faster

Variety: Big data is any type of data - structured and unstructured data such as text, sensor data, audio, video, click streams, log files and more. New insights are found when analyzing these data types together.

- Monitor 100's of live video feeds from surveillance cameras to target points of interest

- Exploit the 80% data growth"

Retrieved from: http://www-01.ibm.com/software/in/data/bigdata, July 2014

The think-tankers on the Executive Leadership Council at Association for Information and Image Management (AIIM) systematically use a four-box matrix to reduce uncertainty, allocate investments and calibrate new product/service initiatives. This simple tool—with "important and difficult" in the upper right and "unimportant and easy" in the lower left—produces surprisingly powerful insights.

During year-end discussions with 40 executives in 20 vertical markets, I discovered that they all now place big data in that upper-right quadrant. Similarly, readers of Booz & Co.'s Strategy+Business blog designated big data the 2013 Strategy of the Year, and the co-directors of Cognizant's Center for the Future of Work, in a masterful white paper, placed big-data-enabled "meaning making" at the pinnacle of strategic endeavor.

Every hour, Walmart controls more than 1 million customer transactions. All of this information is transferred into a database working with over 2.5 petabytes of information. According to FICO, the Credit Card Fraud System currently in place helps protect over 2 billion accounts all over the globe. Currently, Facebook holds more than 45 billion photos in its entire user base, and the number of photos is growing daily. Finally, *The Economist* recently pointed out that we are now able to decode the human genome in under 1 week—where it took 10 years to do so originally.

—Bill Kleyman, "The Big Data Battleground: Analyzing the Big Picture."
Data Source Knowledge, September 2012

According to a study conducted by the International Data Group (IDC) in 2011, growth rates are projected to range from 45—120 percent annually depending on industry and the source of the projection.

Data sources are expanding to include the "Internet of things" One example came from a GE investor conference in June 2014, where the company indicated it's "airplane engines recently started sending in operating data for further analysis. In 2013; GE collected information on 15,000 flights. At about 14 gigabytes of flight metrics per flight, all of this information would fit on a single consumer-grade hard drive." The discussion went on to indicate, "In 2015, the data collection should grow to 10 million flights and 750 hard drives full of operational data. GE has 350 engineers working on analytics for this large and rapidly growing information trove, in conjunction with 25 airlines that have agreed to share this automatically collected information."

—Anders Bylund, "How Will the Internet of Things Help GE?" The Motley Fool, June 2014

According to the Forbes December 2013 edition," IDC predicts spending of more than $14 billion on big data technologies and services or 30% growth year-over-year, 'as demand for big data analytics skills continues to outstrip supply.' The cloud will play a bigger role with IDC predicting a race to develop cloud-based platforms capable of streaming data in real time. There will be increased use by enterprises of externally-sourced data and applications and "data brokers will proliferate." IDC predicts explosive growth in big data analytics services, with the number of providers to triple in three years. 2014 spending on these services will exceed $4.5 billion, growing by 21%.

—Gil Press, "IDC: Top 10 Technology Predictions for 2014", *Forbes December 2013*

How does this focus on big data and analytics impact leaders and their organizations?

As I wrote in *The New Know*, "The days of showing up, of attendance-based compensation, are *over*. The backlash associated with the bonuses paid to financial services executives involved in destabilizing the global financial infrastructure has created an atmosphere of measurement vigilantism. The desire to know will define the next quarter century. In the not-so-distant future, guessing/making things up, not having the right data, or employing the wrong algorithms to data will come to be viewed as termination offenses and egregious social taboos." Your personal and professional success will increasingly come to depend on your ability to collect, organize, analyze, and act on the exponentially increasing mass of information that defines the first moments of the twenty-first century.

The new law of the jungle is: Know and prosper; not know: Wither and die. You are standing at the hinge of history, a true *inflection point*; the choice is yours.

While delivering the true value of big data and analytics is important, it is also difficult. The thing the experts don't tell you is that it takes time. Acquiring the body of knowledge, learning the language, adopting the ideas, and making the cultural adjustments required for harnessing full value from big data is a cumulative process. The path to big data mastery took one entertainment conglomerate seven years—three to decide to do something and four to build out the infrastructure. Chris

Wegrzyn, director of data architecture for the Democratic National Committee, explained to The Huffington Post why the ramp-up to big data mastery took two years for the Obama 2012 campaign: "It's one thing to build up some technology and hire some people. It's another thing entirely to transform how your operation works fundamentally."

During inflection points, organizations have not only the opportunity but the mandate to determine how to invest their transformation money and employee time and energy to create a strategic advantage. Big data and analytics projects are one signification source of strategic advantage but only if done efficiently and effectively. These implementations require highly effective leadership.

Effective leadership drives successful transformation.

Big data and analytics implementations will only be successful if they are aligned with the overall business strategy. Leadership drives the strategic decisions to invest in leadership, how to align these projects with the overall organizational goals, and how to implement the programs efficiently and effectively.

This book provides a pragmatic approach to leading transformations that depend on implementing big data and analytics transformations. It provides tools that help leaders align strategic goals and resources to achieve actionable outcomes. It helps leaders become more innovative so their actions are aligned with the projects they are implementing. They must learn to adapt to the situation, processes, tools, and people to lead new outcomes. They must understand how to create alignment between their own behaviors, the culture they are creating and the analytics programs they are implementing.

As a leader, your legacy is what matters. This book will help you build on your current leadership skills, develop an analytic culture, and implement successful analytics programs that when combined will be your legacy. Reading this book, doing the exercises, and embracing its lessons are great places to start for you to lead your organization to a new outcome.

Thornton A. May is author of The New Know: Innovation Powered by Analytics and *executive director of the IT Leadership Academy at Florida State College in Jacksonville and a regular contributor to Computer World.*

INTRODUCTION
Using Innovative Leadership to Implement Analytics Programs

The Challenge

Organizations are changing how they operate based on large volumes of data and analysis:

> *"It's not only the amount of data, but also the ability to transform their industries that is inspiring organizations to take action. Using big data and analytics, for example, doctors can better diagnose illnesses in order to help save lives. At the same time, financial institutions can analyze big data to detect and prevent fraud. The use of social networks and apps is driving transparent interactions and creating fundamentally new sources of data that didn't exist five years ago. Businesses are learning to harness this data—generated both inside and outside of their organizations. As more organizations embrace big data and analytics, they will continue to find more ways to transform their businesses and acquire, grow and retain their customers."*

> —Inhi Cho Suh, Vice President of Big Data, IBM,
> "Five Ways Companies Can Compete Using Big Data and Analytics", *Forbes April 2014*

This use of big data and the analytics and insights it generates is driving significant organizational transformation not only in IT departments but in how organizations conduct business. It is changing organizational strategy, culture, and how work is conducted. These changes start with successfully implementing big data and analytics projects that then drive, over time, large scale organizational transformation. This workbook is designed to help you think through the analytics implementation, including leadership changes, culture changes, and systemic changes.

> *"Today any company that isn't rethinking its direction at least every few years—as well as constantly adjusting to changing contexts—and then quickly making significant operational changes is putting itself at risk. But, as any number of business leaders can attest, the tension between needing to stay ahead of increasingly fierce competition and needing to deliver this year's results can be overwhelming."*

> —John P. Kotter,
> *Harvard Business Review*, November 2012

Accelerating change continues to impact every facet of business. To thrive long term, business leaders must make implementing change as a core competency, developing an organization that is Agile and can continually not only adapt but lead and drive required changes including making cultural shifts. Building this capacity will enable them to capitalize on our changing world instead of merely attempting to adapt to it.

In attempts to stay abreast of rapid changes, continuous advancements in systems' efficiencies have been enabled by unprecedented rates of technology development. The ensuing race to keep pace with competitors and technology has proven deeply problematic, as innovating functional efficiencies has become the singular focus of corporate strategy at the expense of vision and cultural cohesion. Significant dissonance between day-to-day function and purpose has arisen as companies have focused their energies on performance training rather than the development of sophisticated thinking, complex interaction capabilities, or comprehensive decision-making skills. In essence, organizational strategy has been reduced to improving functional processes, and technical competency has inappropriately become equivalent to strategic vision. While companies recognize they must align technology with business imperatives, this is easier said than done. This alignment requires formulation of relationships, ability to influence and understanding of industry domains.

This shallow version of strategy has not only driven market volatility, it has worked to marginalize new organizational strategies--particularly those emerging to address the flattening global economy. Companies are applying more technological innovation to resolve issues that were created by a myopic focus on innovating technology. These technological innovations include an exponentially growing interest in "big data" and analytics.

Organizations need innovation to successfully navigate the new economic landscape—and they are not getting it. It's relatively rare for transformation programs to deliver the results that were projected in the original business case.

> *According to the Standish Group, which measures performance success in IT projects, more than 60% of the IT projects conducted in 2010 failed to deliver on their goals because they either came in late or over budget, or they had fewer features than were originally specified. Since global investments in IT will total more than $2 trillion in 2012, according to Forrester Research, the total cost of this wasted effort is substantial.*

> —Steve Berez, Stephen Phillips and Jean-Claude Ramirez
> "Five Keys to IT Program Success", *Bain Industry Brief,* June 2012

Simply put, companies attempting to traverse the new economic landscape with incomplete tactics will not succeed. We integrate these findings and others into our recommendations throughout this book. In addition to looking at tactics used to implement change, we also need to look at the impact leadership has on the organization's ability to successfully implement change.

More comprehensive approaches to leadership and organizational transformation must be seriously considered. An exclusive focus on systems' performance and analytics can prove costly. Enhancing organizational capacity must extend beyond increasing system functionality.

Change-management processes supplement the system we know. They can slide easily into a project-management organization. They can be made stronger or faster by adding more resources, more sophisticated versions of the same old methods, or smarter people to drive the process—but again—only up to a point. After that point, using this approach to launch strategic initiatives that ask an organization to absorb more change faster can create confusion, resistance, fatigue, and higher costs.

—John P. Kotter,
"Accelerate," *Harvard Business Review*, November 2012

If, in addition to developing better functional processes, *you also begin to clarify strategic vision, grow leadership capacity, and build a cohesive company culture—you will achieve much greater and more sustainable success.*

Of course not every challenge requires a leader to change how he thinks about the organization or himself as a leader to "solve" it, but many complex challenges do. One of the biggest challenges for today's leader is developing the ability to identify which problems require complex solutions and which ones are merely technical in nature and can be solved using more traditional approaches. Developing complex solutions requires experimentation and often generates new discoveries. These solutions can take a long time to implement and are rarely successfully implemented by edict. To succeed in developing complex solutions, leaders need to fully understand the organization's problems and challenges and their own leadership capabilities along with understanding the barriers and resistance they will likely face.

> The change process works on the leader (requires them to change to lead the evolving organization) at the same time the leader works on the change.

Complex challenges illuminate deeply held beliefs and force not only a change in how work is done, but also in the leaders themselves and an organization's values. What results is more than a process change or innovation translation. A complex solution will create changes in processes, but also in personal beliefs, behaviors, and interactions. Solutions to complex challenges that are most effective are those that change the leader and the organization's *relationship* to processes, values, behaviors, and interactions. In other words, the change process works on the leader (requires them to change to lead the evolving organization) at the same time the leader works on the change. This change could involve building new technical skills or it could actually involve the leader changing how he looks at a segment of the overall organization and how he leads. An example of this is leaders who are now encouraging employees to build stronger professional relations in the workplace to promote employee engagement.

Leaders must be willing to face what they will need to change about themselves as well as change about their organizations to successfully solve adaptive challenges.

—Ronald A. Heifetz and Donald A. Laurie,
"The Work of Leadership," *Harvard Business Review Breakthrough Leadership*, December 2001

As the term suggests, "adaptive challenges" require leaders and employees to learn new ways of thinking about the work as well as new ways of doing the work. Adaptive challenges are often the most elusive as they require that we change not only the organization but take on the difficult process of looking at ourselves as leaders and determine how we need to change in order to solve the challenges we are facing.

We will use the terms "adaptive change" and "transformation" throughout this workbook to mean complex changes that require a solution involving change to the leader, the culture, and the organizational systems. Heifetz and Laurie built on these initial findings in their June 2009 book, The Practice of Adaptive Leadership: Tools and Tactics for Changing Your Organization and the World. Now that you understand the magnitude of this issue, we can discuss the systematic approach to implementation.

The Solution

This workbook is based on a synthesis of several models and the principles they put forth into a process and series of questions a leader can ask to guide his actions when dealing with adaptive challenges created by the increased predictive power of well implemented analytics programs.

Jim Collins, the bestselling business author of *Good to Great* and *Great by Choice*, talks about leadership being critical to effectively move organizations to greatness. He uses terms like Level 5 Leader and 10x Leader to refer to the type of leadership required to successfully implement adaptive change. In his books, Collins starts with leadership as the foundation for effective transformation.

According to Kotter, one of the five principles of accelerating change is:

> "...much more leadership, not just more management. At the core of a successful hierarchy is competent management. A strategy network, by contrast, needs lots of leadership, which means it operates with different processes and language and expectations. The game is all about vision, opportunity, agility, inspired action, and celebration—not project management, budget reviews, reporting relationships, compensation, and accountability to a plan...The new operating system continually assesses the business, the industry, and the organization, and reacts with greater agility, speed, and creativity than the existing one. It complements rather than overburdens the traditional hierarchy, thus freeing the latter to do what it's optimized to do. It actually makes enterprises easier to run and accelerates strategic change. This is not an 'either or' idea. It's 'both and.' I'm proposing two systems that operate in concert."

> —John P. Kotter,
> "Accelerate!," *Harvard Business Review*, November 2012

Kotter's concept of a dual operating system moving beyond hierarchy to a networked model of operation is addressed in our Innovative Leadership Model.

Innovative Leadership and the Art of Leading Change

The concept of leading change starts with leadership. Yet in many organizations, the process of leading change often omits the idea that transforming leaders is part of the overall analytics transformation process. This book starts with an approach to leadership that we call Innovative Leadership. It is a comprehensive model defining the five key elements required to successfully address adaptive challenges and transform organizations to solve these challenges.

- Leadership Behaviors
- Situational Analysis
- Resilience
- Developmental Perspective
- Leader Type

Leveraging the focus of key researchers along with our change implementation experience, we focus on building Innovative Leadership as the foundation for implementing adaptive change. This ability is developed by addressing the five elements in the image to the left.

Innovative Leadership is also based on the recognition that four dimensions (intention, behavior, culture, and systems) exist in all experiences and already influence every interactive experience we have. To deny the interplay of any one of the four dimensions is to miss the full picture. You can only build Innovative Leadership by simultaneously addressing all four dimensions.

Because Innovative Leadership influences by engaging the four dimensions equally, innovative leaders are uniquely qualified to implement adaptive change with a much higher success rate. A primary reason for transformation failure is that leaders focus primarily on the systems, rather than the larger context that includes themselves as leader and the organizational culture.

Benefits

By combining Innovative Leadership with a comprehensive change model where the leader equally considers the four dimensions, implementing transformative change to solve adaptive problems will have a higher success rate. This higher success rate is possible because this new model accomplishes the following:

- Addresses adaptive problems by analyzing them and developing comprehensive solutions beyond those found in traditional problem-solving approaches

- Addresses the four dimensions: a leader's intention and behavior along with the organization's culture and systems in a systematic manner that creates alignment between them

- Includes the innovative leader in the change process: expecting the leader to innovate how they lead to keep pace with the challenges they are solving

During this era of increased complexity, an accelerated need for change, and failed change initiatives, it is critical for organizations to identify new models which address these challenges while concurrently maintaining efficient and effective operations and have a higher likelihood of yielding successful and sustained change.

This model (shown below) is based on a combination of approaches, including Kotter's model in *Leading Change*, Heifitz and Laurie's model from their paper "The Work of Leadership," and Ken Wilber's integral model. While our model appears to be linear in nature, the timing may not be as steps may happen concurrently—and in some cases are repeated for multiple audiences—and one step may not be complete when another is started.

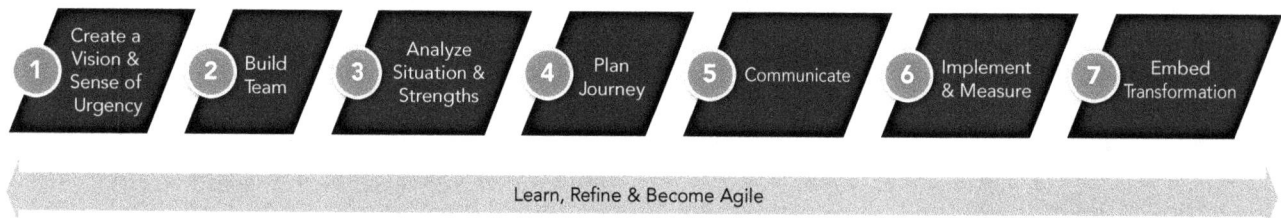

Implementing substantial analytics projects and the associated business transformation is the work of innovative leaders, leading a skilled team of people, to accomplish a goal that will become more finely tuned during the implementation process. To add to the complexity, these programs are more successful when implemented outside of the corporate hierarchy, using networks of people and projects that are interdependent of one another. The purpose of this book is to give you—as an innovative leader—a high-level understanding of the change process and how to lead change; it is not intended to teach you the nuts and bolts of how to manage the program or the change effort as part of the program team.

Special note from the authors

While this model appears to be linear, it can be used sequentially with overlapping steps, or the concepts and tasks can be applied in an Agile manner. The sequential approach will provide a logical foundation that will continue to grow throughout the process. For organizations that have adopted Agile methodologies, this model includes many techniques and templates that will help your enterprise increase commitment and adopt the analytic models your teams create. The first chapter is your leadership foundation to ensure your success.

REFLECTION QUESTIONS

Each chapter in this workbook contains exercises designed to help you apply what you learn to your analytics projects immediately. Following is a list of questions designed to help you start thinking about how this content will apply to your immediate work.

Are our efforts to implement analytics programs considered adaptive challenges?

■■■■■■

How does your organization integrate leadership development into the transformation process?

■■■■■■

What is your leadership role in implementing change?

■■■■■■

Do you have any experience in aligning an organization across the four domains, your intention and action, the organization's culture and systems?

Defining an Innovative Leader

Because Innovative Leadership is a critical foundation to this model, we want to start with the definition. What are specific qualities that differentiate an innovative leader from a traditional leader? In this era of rapid business, social, and ecological change, a successful innovative leader is a leader who can consistently:

- Clarify and effectively articulate vision
- Link that vision to attainable strategic initiatives
- Develop self and influence the development of other leaders
- Build effective teams by helping colleagues realize and act on their own leadership strengths
- Cultivate alliances and partnerships
- Anticipate and aggressively respond both to challenges and opportunities
- Develop robust and resilient solutions
- Develop and test hypotheses
- Measure, learn, and refine on an ongoing basis

To further illustrate some of the qualities of Innovative Leadership, we offer this comparison between traditional leadership and innovative leadership:

TRADITIONAL LEADERSHIP	INNOVATIVE LEADERSHIP
Leader is guided primarily by desire for personal success and peripherally by organizational success	Leader is humbly guided by a more integrated vision of success based on both personal and organizational performance and the value of the organization's positive impact to both
Leader decides in a "command and control" style; leader has all the answers	Leader leverages team for answers as part of the decision-making process while still maintaining active involvement
Leader picks a direction in "black/white" manner, tends to dogmatically stay the course	Leader perceives and behaves like a scientist: continually experimenting, measuring, and testing for improvement and exploring new models and approaches
Leader focuses on being technically correct and in control	Leader is continually learning and developing self and others
Leader manages people to perform by being autocratic and controlling	Leader motivates people to perform through strategic focus, mentoring and coaching, and interpersonal intelligence
Leader tends to the numbers and primarily utilizes quantitative measures that drive those numbers	Leader tends to financial performance, customer satisfaction, employee engagement, community impact, and cultural cohesion using both quantitative and qualitative measures

Getting the Most from the Workbook

Before you get started, take a moment to think about why you purchased this workbook. Setting goals and understanding your intentions and expectations about the exercises will help you identify and drive your desired results.

In order to help clarify, consider writing your answers to the following questions:

> Learning Practices are actions you can take to accelerate and enhance experiential learning and determine whether you proactively pursue learning in your day-to-day work life, or focus only on getting the job done.

- What are the five to seven events and choices that brought you to where you are professionally and personally?

- What stands out in the list you have made? Are there any surprises or patterns?

- How did these events and choices contribute to choosing to buy and use this workbook?

- What do you hope to gain from your investment in leadership development?

- What meaningful impact will it have professionally and personally?

In addition to reflecting on the questions, we recommend you use the Learning Practices to help you get the most out of this investment in your development. It is our experience that people who adhere to the following practices tend to have a deeper and more enriching overall experience, and more effectively take advantage of what this workbook has to offer.

What are "Learning Practices"?

Now that you have purchased this workbook, you may be wondering, "What can I actually do to get better as a leader?" It's one thing to know that you need to "think more strategically," or improve at "giving performance feedback and coaching" to your direct reports. It's something completely different to translate that into practical actions that bring about lasting change, growth, and development.

Since most of us spend over ninety percent of our work time actually working rather than in training programs or workshops, time on the job and our day-to-day experiences are our best and most accessible opportunities to learn. We just need to know how to use our experience to grow and develop.

Learning Practices are actions you can take to accelerate and enhance experiential learning and determine whether you proactively pursue learning in your day-to-day work life, or focus only on getting the job done. According to Steve Terrell's research with leaders, those who consistently and rigorously use the Learning Practices learn significantly more and faster while achieving better results. The following key Learning Practices have significant potential for growing and accelerating your ability to learn from experience:

LEARNING PRACTICES	RELATED ACTION OF BEHAVIOR
1. Take responsibility for your own learning and development	Be 100% responsible for the outcome of your engagement with this material
2. Approach new assignments/ opportunities with openness to experience and positive intention to learn	Each assignment will provide you with opportunities to learn things you did not know about yourself or others; take advantage of these opportunities even if you think you might already know the answers
3. Seek and use feedback	Identify who will provide you with feedback and use what you learn about yourself to learn and grow (see chapter on building your team)
4. Develop a clear understanding of I your strengths and areas of development	Determine which assessments will give you the most valuable set of feedback (see chapter on analyzing your strengths and situation)
5. Ask great questions and demonstrate curiosity and lean into optimal discomfort; take risks without overwhelming yourself	Remain openly curious through the process; ongoing learning is an important key to success in leadership development. Be candid, open, and direct. Allow yourself to be curious and vulnerable
6. Listen in a manner that leaves you open to personal transformation	Listen intently, deeply, and empathically, identifying ways to not only change your behavior, but also how you see the world
7. Respond to experience with adaptability and flexibility	Your ability to respond to unexpected situations with finesse will position you well during your development process (see resilience element in Innovative Leadership)
8. Actively reflect and practice mindfulness	Take the time to answer the refection questions and be fully present while you are doing the exercises
9. Actively experiment with new approaches to learning	Find opportunities where you can safely apply new ways of learning skills or behaviors such as special programs or volunteer roles
10. Closely observe and learn from others	Find a mentor or person you believe has mastered the skills you are trying to develop and closely observe what this person does and how they do it. Try to "steal" or adopt the techniques they use to succeed
11. Participate as fully as possible	Complete all the exercises to the best of your abilities. Apply the concepts and skills that work best for you, and modify those that do not
12. Practice good life management	Invest time at scheduled intervals to work on the materials when you are mentally and emotionally at your best
13. Take the process seriously, and more importantly take yourself lightly. Make this a positive and rewarding experience	Allow yourself balance. Find the lesson and humor in both your successes and mistakes. Most importantly, have fun!

Recommended Uses of This Guide To Develop the Learning Mindset

1. Turn the switch to "on." Decide that you want to develop the Learning Mindset and commit to making it an area of your ongoing growth and development.

2. Be intentional about learning. Use "preflection," orienting yourself toward learning every day by thinking about and envisioning in advance what you want to learn. Use reflection by replaying the day's events in your mind and thinking about what you learned.

3. Use mantras to reprogram your autopilot. All of us operate on autopilot most of the time. This is both a good thing and a bad thing. While it helps to automate repetitive tasks and actions so we don't have to think about them, it also leads to a lack of attention to important information in the world around us. On autopilot, we work on the basis of old assumptions, beliefs, and data. If you want to start learning more from experience, find your own personal mantra to orient your mind toward learning. Here are a few examples:

   a. "Development is about getting better and better, not being perfect."

   b. "Never give up."

   c. "It's not whether I win or lose. I win if I learn, grow, and develop."

   d. "Observe. Learn. Improve. Getting better."

4. Fake It 'til You Make It. If it doesn't seem natural to you to go through your day with an eye toward learning, one way to counter is to repeatedly and consciously do things that someone with a strong Learning Mindset would do. For example, purposely seek out new experiences that take you out of your comfort zone, and when engaging in those experiences make it your goal to learn as much as you can. Over time, you will begin to develop new neural pathways that contribute to new habits of mind and behavior: The Learning Mindset.

To begin using Learning Practices as tools to accelerate and enhance your experiential learning, start with taking responsibility for your own growth and development. Until you actually ***own*** your development—***taking, not just accepting, responsibility*** for your own learning and growth—you are a passive bystander who is waiting or sleep-walking through life. Unless you take responsibility for your own growth and development, learning may or may not happen, and, if it does, it will accidental, incidental, serendipitous, and tacit. You will therefore be missing out on the biggest developmental arena available to leaders: day-to-day work experience.

As you face the challenges of global leaders, remember that the most effective leaders have the ability to transform their experiences into growth and development. The greater the challenge, the more significant is the opportunity to develop as a leader. If you have a Learning Mindset and consistently and rigorously put Learning Practices into action, you will learn significantly more, faster, and as a result you'll perform at a higher level—creating greater value for your company and for yourself.

Adopting the Learning Mindset and using Learning Practices is not as simple as it may seem, and as Benjamin Franklin put it in his *New Farmer's Almanac,* "There are three things extremely hard: steel, a diamond, and to know one's self."

On the surface, the logic is clear: attitudes lead to behaviors. And, you may already be thinking, "Of course, I have a Learning Mindset! I do some of those Learning Practices all the time!" Unfortunately, most of us do a poor job of assessing our own competencies and capabilities. Many of us tend to exaggerate our strengths and downplay our weaknesses. We all need to use a heightened level of self-examination and conduct an honest appraisal of ourselves as we work on developing ourselves as leaders.

How to Use the Workbook

Each chapter of the workbook builds on a series of exercises and reflection questions designed to guide you through the process of developing your own abilities as an innovative leader. We recommend that you use the following sequence to efficiently process the material:

1. Read Intently

Read through the chapter completely as we introduce and illustrate an integrated set of concepts for each element in building Innovative Leadership.

2. Contemplate

Using a set of carefully chosen applications and specifically designed exercises will help to bring the concepts to life. Through a process of dynamic examination and reflection, you will be encouraged to contemplate some significant, real-life implications of change. Many of the exercises can be done on your own; others are designed to be conducted with input from your colleagues.

3. Link Together Your Experience

As you sequentially build your understanding, you will begin noticing habits and conditioned patterns that present you with clear opportunities for growth. Though you may encounter personal resistance along the way, you will also discover new and exciting strengths. As you become more adept at using these ideas, you will find yourself increasingly capable of proactive engagement with the concepts, along with an ability to respond to situations requiring Innovative Leadership with greater capacity.

Once you have completed the process, you will have created a plan to grow as an innovative global leader and transform your organization using analytics as the catalyst.

Chapter One of the workbook is focused on individual leadership to help you build an understanding of what Innovative Leadership is and how you can apply it to solve adaptive problems. We explore each of the five elements in detail and give examples of how you, as an innovative leader, can use these elements in your transformation effort.

Chapters Two through Eight focus on the process of leading transformative change to address adaptive challenges specifically focused on implementing analytics as a means to transform an organization. This section puts Innovative Leadership to work by building on what we learned in Chapter One. It provides a change model and gives an example of how an innovative leader implements transformative change. It is designed to offer a change model and practical tools and steps that you can use to lead change.

Leadership Behaviors

Situational Analysis

Resilience

Developmental Perspective

Leader Type

SECTION I

The Art of Leadership

Chapter One: "Five Elements of Innovative Leadership" explores the five elements of Innovative Leadership in greater depth (reflected in the graphic above). You will be using them as an individual leader, in your work with the leadership team, and also in the organization as you implement transformative change.

This chapter offers a definition of the key element, explains the role it plays in using Innovative Leadership to transform organizations, and gives an example of the models we use. These five key elements are interconnected and must be considered as a whole to build truly Innovative Leadership.

This model also serves as the foundation in Chapters Two through Eight, in which you will put your Innovative Leadership skills to work as you implement your analytics programs.

Score Yourself on Awareness of Leader Type and Self-Management

Think about how you responded to work situations over the past year and answer the following questions using this scale:

Never (1)　　*Rarely (2)*　　*Sometimes (3)*　　*Often (4)*　　*Almost always (5)*

1. I have taken a leadership type assessment such as the Enneagram, Myers-Briggs Type Indicator, or DiSC, and used this information about myself to increase my effectiveness.　　**1 2 3 4 5**

2. I use the insight from this assessment to understand my type. Specifically, I understand my gifts and limitations, and try to leverage my strengths and manage my limitations.　　**1 2 3 4 5**

3. I have a reflection practice where I understand, actively monitor, and work with my "fixations" (negative thought patterns).　　**1 2 3 4 5**

4. I have a clear sense of who I am and what I contribute to the world.　　**1 2 3 4 5**

5. I manage my emotional reactions to allow me to respond with socially appropriate behavior.　　**1 2 3 4 5**

6. I am aware of what causes me stress and actively manage it.　　**1 2 3 4 5**

7. I have positive coping strategies.　　**1 2 3 4 5**

8. I actively seek ways to feel empowered even when the organization may not empower me.　　**1 2 3 4 5**

Total Score

- If your overall score in this category is 24 or less, it's time to pay attention to your leadership type and self-management.

- If your overall score in this category is 25 to 31, you are in the healthy range, but could still benefit from some focus on your leadership type and self-management.

- If your overall score is 32 or above, congratulations! You are self-aware and using your leadership type to increase your effectiveness.

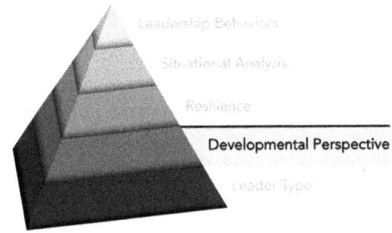

Score Yourself on Developmental Perspective Aligned with Innovation

Think about how you responded to work situations over the past year and answer the following questions using this scale:

Never (1)   Rarely (2)   Sometimes (3)   Often (4)   Almost always (5)

1. I have a sense of life purpose and do work that is generally aligned with that purpose.   **1 2 3 4 5**

2. I am motivated by the impact I make on the world more than on personal notoriety.   **1 2 3 4 5**

3. I try to live my life according to my personal values.   **1 2 3 4 5**

4. I believe that collaboration across groups, organizations, and cultures is important to accomplish our goals.   **1 2 3 4 5**

5. I believe that getting business results must be balanced with treating people fairly and kindly.   **1 2 3 4 5**

6. I consistently seek input from others to test my thinking and expand my perspective.   **1 2 3 4 5**

7. I think about the impact of my work on my community and the world.   **1 2 3 4 5**

8. I am open and curious, always trying new things and learning from all of them.   **1 2 3 4 5**

9. I appreciate the value of rules and am willing to question them in a professional manner.   **1 2 3 4 5**

Total Score

- If your overall score in this category is 27 or less, it's time to pay attention to your developmental level, including testing your current level and focusing on developing in the area of developmental perspectives.

- If your overall score in this category is 28 to 35, you are in the healthy range, but could still benefit from some focus on developing in the area of developmental perspectives.

- If your score is 36 or above, congratulations! Your developmental level appears to be aligned with innovate leadership, yet this assessment is only a subset of a full assessment.

Score Yourself on Resilience

Think about how you responded to work situations over the past year and answer the following questions using this scale:

Never (1)   Rarely (2)   Sometimes (3)   Often (4)   Almost always (5)

1. I consistently take care of my physical needs such as getting enough sleep and exercise.   1 2 3 4 5

2. I have a sense of purpose and get to do activities that contribute to that purpose daily.   1 2 3 4 5

3. I have a high degree of self-awareness and actively manage my thoughts.   1 2 3 4 5

4. I have a strong support system consisting of a healthy mix of friends, colleagues, and family.   1 2 3 4 5

5. I can reframe challenges to find something of value in most situations.   1 2 3 4 5

6. I build strong trusting relationships at work with a broad range of people.   1 2 3 4 5

7. I am aware of my own "self-talk" and actively manage it.   1 2 3 4 5

8. I have a professional development plan that includes gaining skills and additional perspectives from a broad range of people who think and act differently than I do.   1 2 3 4 5

Total Score

- If your overall score in this category is 24 or less, it's time to pay attention to your resilience.

- If your overall score in this category is 25 to 31, you are in the healthy range, but could still benefit from some focus on resilience.

- If your score is 32 or above, congratulations! Although this assessment is only a subset of the full resilience assessment, you are likely performing well in the area of resilience.

Score Yourself on Situational Analysis

Think about how you responded to work situations over the past year and answer the following questions using this scale:

Never (1)   Rarely (2)   Sometimes (3)   Often (4)   Almost always (5)

1. I am aware of my own passions and values.   1 2 3 4 5

2. My behavior consistently reflects my goals and values.   1 2 3 4 5

3. I feel safe pushing back when I am asked to do things that are not aligned with   1 2 3 4 5
    my values.

4. I am aware that my behavior and decisions as a leader have an impact on the   1 2 3 4 5
    people I work with (even if I am not directly managing them/others).

5. I am deliberate about aligning my behaviors with the behaviors the   1 2 3 4 5
    organization values, and I pay attention to delivering the desired results
    (both results and behaviors).

6. I am aware of how my values align with those of the organization and where   1 2 3 4 5
    they are misaligned; if there are misalignments, I try to find constructive ways
    to address these differences. I am also aware that organization values and
    behaviors may differ across countries.

Total Score

- If your overall score in this category is 18 or less, it's time to pay attention to your alignment with the organization and also the alignment of culture and systems within the organization that you are able to impact.

- If your overall score in this category is 19 to 23, you are in the healthy range, but could still benefit from some focus on alignment.

- If your score is 24 or above, congratulations! You are well aligned with the organization, and the organization's culture and systems are well-aligned.

Score Yourself on Leadership Behaviors

Think about how you responded to work situations over the past year and answer the following questions using this scale:

Never (1)   Rarely (2)   Sometimes (3)   Often (4)   Almost always (5)

1. I tend to be proactive. I anticipate what is coming next and actively manage it. **1 2 3 4 5**

2. I focus on creating results in a way that helps me grow and develop along with those who work for me while accomplishing our tasks. **1 2 3 4 5**

3. I think about the impact of my actions on the organization rather than just getting the job done. **1 2 3 4 5**

4. I see how my work contributes to organizational success. **1 2 3 4 5**

5. I deliberately try to improve myself and the organization. **1 2 3 4 5**

6. I take time to mentor others, even when I am busy (this could be formal or informal mentoring). **1 2 3 4 5**

7. I consider myself to be a personal learner and I invest time reading and trying new ideas and activities. I am curious. **1 2 3 4 5**

8. I have the courage to speak out in a professional manner when asked to do something with which I disagree. **1 2 3 4 5**

9. I accomplish results by working with and through others in a positive, constructive, and culturally sensitive manner. **1 2 3 4 5**

Total Score

- If your overall score in this category is 27 or less, it's time to pay attention to your alignment with the organization and also the alignment of culture and systems within the organization that you are able to impact.

- If your overall score in this category is 28 to 35, you are in the healthy range, but could still benefit from some focus on alignment.

- If your score is 36 or above, congratulations! You are well aligned with the organization, and the organization's culture and systems are well-aligned.

CHAPTER 1
FIVE ELEMENTS OF INNOVATIVE LEADERSHIP

Leadership Behaviors

Situational Analysis

Resilience

Developmental Perspective

Leader Type

Figure 1.1 Five Elements of Innovative Leadership

Leader Type

Sarah was the vice president of marketing for a Fortune 100 company when we met several years ago. She was easily recognizable throughout her division for the bright colors that she wore and for her equally bright disposition, and her ability to make people feel instantly comfortable, acknowledged, and appreciated. Sarah rose through the ranks in the company, starting out as a sales assistant, and then slowly earning her way to progressively more responsibility. As an executive, she was centered, focused, and highly successful. Her office was an interesting fusion of beautifully crafted cherry furniture, professional certifications and awards, and personal memorabilia honoring both work and family relationships. The office was neatly organized despite that it was obviously well-used.

After first courteously asking about my work and my family, her demeanor became serious. "I wanted to meet with you today because I am very concerned about one of my senior directors," she began. "He was a top salesman when he came to us and was quickly moved into our high-achievers program. His numbers were always solid and his group was very productive when he was a manager." At that, she looked down reflectively and then back to me. "But even then" she remarked, "I would hear about incidents where people left meetings feeling demoralized. He has such strong people skills and is so bright; I thought that these incidents must have been attempts to help his staff stretch. Now, in retrospect, I think I missed some warning signs. We are at the point where he has stepped on so many toes that nobody wants to work with him."

Sarah's posture shifted and she leaned into the conversation. "Even worse," she said emphatically, "he seems totally unaware that his behaviors and decision-making style put people off. After talking with him and several members of his team, I've realized that he feels that his charm and intelligence are all that he needs. He really has no idea that he is burning important bridges. Right now, he continues to put his career at risk and will certainly make his—in fact, our—long-term success unattainable." She sat silently for a moment as she collected her final thoughts, then asked, "Is there any way that you can help him become self-aware enough to resurrect his reputation?"

Of course there was. Yet, problems like those of this senior director are as complex as they are common. He had all of the technical skills, intelligence, and the motivation to be an effective leader. However, staff turnover, poor collaboration, and a reputation of being difficult to work with find him doing as much harm to his company as good. And worst of all, he was totally unaware of how his manner and behavior negatively affected those with whom he worked. Coaching Sarah and her problem director—preferentially with her entire management team—through the Leadership Development process and the five elements of Innovative Leadership would bring everyone clarity on their own strengths and weaknesses as well as building a stronger team.

The Importance of Leader Type

Part of the challenge in building Innovative Leadership is learning to leverage the clarity of your introspection. Looking inside yourself and examining the make-up of your inner being enables you to function in a highly-grounded way, rather than operating from the innate biases of more uninformed decision-making.

First and foremost start by simply considering your disposition, tendencies, inclinations, and ways of being. Innovative Leadership hinges on understanding the simple, native manner in which you show up in your life. One way to observe this is by examining key aspects of your inner being, often called Leader Type, which reflect the leader's personality type. The Leader Personality Type (going forward referred to as Leader Type) critically influences who you are as a leader. It is an essential foundation of your personal make-up and greatly shapes the effectiveness of your leadership. The ancient adage "know thyself" holds true as a crucial underpinning in leadership performance.

> Your ability to use deep introspection relies on your development of, and capacity for, self-understanding and self-awareness.

When the sixty-five member Advisory Council for the Stanford Graduate School of Business were polled several years ago on the topic of what was most important to include in the school's curriculum, there was an overwhelming—and quite impressive—agreement that the most important thing business school graduates needed to learn was self-awareness and the resultant ability to reduce denial in their perceptions of themselves and their actions. All the tools of the MBA trade—forecasting, strategic planning, and financial analysis, among many others—were less important to learn than the skill of self-awareness and the ability to reduce denial. This speaks to the emerging deep recognition that we are highlighting in Innovative Leadership: leaders, through their own personality quirks and biases, can derail the most progressive initiatives toward an organization's sustainable success.

Your ability to use deep introspection relies on your development of, and capacity for, self-understanding and self-awareness. Both allow you profound openness of personal perspective as well as a greater understanding of others. These critical traits support leaders' abilities to self-regulate, communicate effectively with others, and encourage personal learning. Employing a deeper understanding of Leader Type for both yourself and others is a powerful tool to promote effective leadership.

It is important to keep in mind that this particular notion of type is inherent to your being and generally does not change significantly over the course of your life. This is an essential point: by ascertaining the distinct "shape" of your type, as well as that of others around you, you can begin to see situations without the bias of your own perceptions. You are then in a better position to leverage what you and others actually demonstrate, rather than acting from speculation. You learn to deeply understand the inner shifts in your strengths, weaknesses, and core patterns. Typing tools are helpful in promoting this kind of self-knowledge and pattern recognition.

> Self-awareness and the capacity for self-management are foundational to Innovative Leadership and overall leadership effectiveness.

By learning about these patterns, you can gain perspective on your life and start connecting the dots among your different experiences. Most of us have a concept about how we behave, but that idea is likely clouded and not entirely true. One of the hardest things for most people is to see themselves accurately. How astonishing it is to see through the clouds and recognize yourself clearly.

—Roxanne Howe Murphy,
Deep Living, 2013

Learning at this deeper level as patterns appear within your immediate experience can offer remarkable insights about areas of life that, in your personal experience, you may tend to exaggerate or overemphasize.

Self-awareness and the capacity for self-management are foundational to Innovative Leadership and overall leadership effectiveness. By becoming aware of your inherent gifts as well as those of others, you are able to improve your personal effectiveness and the personal effectiveness of the teams and departments with which you work.

The key to identifying a person's core type is to look beyond behavior to the factors motivating that behavior. Through awareness of motivation, we can predict the ways in which leaders and organizations sabotage their best efforts, as well as find the line of least resistance toward getting back on track.

Self-awareness, the practice of engaging in self-reflection and achieving clarity of insight, being conscious of one's own identity, and the extent to which perceptions about oneself are accurate and compatible with others' observations, play a pivotal role in leadership. Self-aware leaders self-regulate cognitions, emotions, and behavior more effectively depending on the situation, evaluate their impact on others, and possess higher levels of emotional intelligence.

Thus, they become more versatile in their leadership and may perform better. Consequently, successful leader development is foremost personal development.

—Hilke Richmer, Ed.D. An Analysis of the Effects of Enneagram-Based Leader Development on Self-Awareness: A Case Study At A Midwest Utility Company Doctoral Dissertation, Spalding University. 2011.

Type and Team Effectiveness

Organizations have "personality" types too. This is just another way to think about the organizational culture: the mission or role the organization seeks to fulfill, the favored strategies for accomplishing goals, the behaviors that are rewarded and those that are not, and the subtle hiring filters that tend to screen out people who do not fit. The senior leaders of the organization may or may not reflect the culture. It is immensely valuable for leaders to determine their organization's personality type to be able to harness the natural strengths of that pattern and avoid the imbedded tendencies that create problems. Leaders are likely to have a strong influence on the development of organizational culture, but without clear awareness they may not realize how the leader and the group are aligned and how they sometimes work in opposition.

Research Using Type for Leadership Development and Organizational Effectiveness

Richmer used the Enneagram, a typing model, as the foundation to create a leadership development program and wrote about the results for her doctoral dissertation. According to Richmer:

> The purpose of the research was to assess the effects of the Personal Awareness and Effective Leadership Program in a medium-sized utility company in the Midwest United States. To provide middle managers with a unique development opportunity to enhance their awareness of self and others, the company had customized the Personal Awareness and Effective Leadership Program based on the Enneagram in 2009. The program was implemented in 2010.

> The company's organization development team conceived a program that focused on strengthening middle managers' interpersonal effectiveness and leadership versatility. Considering the extensive practical leadership experience of most middle managers and the challenge of actually changing leadership behavior, the team decided on a novel approach. Team members identified the Enneagram, one of the most comprehensive models of personality [Leader Type] and human development, as an appropriate instrument for the developmental program.

> The Enneagram represented an accepted system to support middle managers to develop a better understanding of themselves and others. Therefore, teaching the Enneagram in leader development should foster middle managers' self-awareness and ultimately advance leadership behavior. This research evaluated the effects of the 2010 Personal Awareness and Effective Leadership Program for middle managers on enhancing self-awareness.

> As a result of participating in the Personal Awareness and Effective Leadership Program, the company expected leaders to (a) understand the Enneagram and the nine [leader] personality types as identified by the Enneagram, be able to identify their

own type, and realize their developmental path, (b) apply Enneagram and Situational Leadership knowledge in their leadership to better recognize motivations and values in themselves and others, and (c) become better equipped to consciously self-regulate behavior in leadership situations and communicate more effectively.

Her research concluded the following:

> *Participants in both cohorts [training groups] found the Enneagram valuable to understand the rationale for their own behavior as well as others' actions and reactions. Participants acknowledged that the Enneagram fostered the understanding of why we behave as we do and also how to best read others. One participant stated that to be an effective leader in today's workforce, you must be able to understand why you are the way you are, so that you can improve.*

> To begin increasing your capacity for clear decision-making, you must first learn to impartially evaluate and examine the intentional and behavioral patterns in yourself as well as others.

Richmer's experiment illustrates a crucial step toward building Innovative Leadership. To begin increasing your capacity for clear decision-making, you must first learn to impartially evaluate and examine the intentional and behavioral patterns in yourself as well as others. The inherent leverage within this simple yet powerful understanding cannot be overstated. It elicits a clarity that will help you make decisions without being governed by the bias of your own perceptions, even as you naturally experience them in any given occasion.

This objectivity is rooted in your ability to see your conditioning without preference. It is this nonjudgmental perspective that allows the nuances of experience to persist in the interest of gaining real understanding. When you begin seeing in this way, you can navigate skillfully and execute without the baggage of erroneous or false expectations.

It is important to note that while assessments can be powerful, in some cases assessments—including the Enneagram—may be used ineffectively. It is critical for you, as leader, to understand how and when to use them before using them. Whatever typing tool is employed, it should always be used to **support and enhance awareness and appreciation of yourself and others.** We have seen highly effective leaders of all personality types, so it is important to note that we are not recommending this tool to screen type for hiring or job placement within leadership roles and, obviously, it is unethical to use assessments to pigeon-hole, label, discriminate, or disadvantage people. Typing assessments are offered to benefit the individual and the team with personal growth and enhanced team effectiveness. We recommend that you share your Enneagram type with team members and colleagues to improve team and group dynamics. The Enneagram is an effective tool to improve self-awareness and social interactions. We have learned that some types are perceived, often inaccurately, as more effective leaders. An example of this is the charismatic leader. The most effective leaders leverage their innate skills and find environments in which they thrive. Additionally, mature leaders often need to function outside of their comfort zone and to do this; they expand their innate capacity so they can be effective in a broad range of environments and situations.

> Whatever typing tool is employed, it should always be used to support and enhance awareness and appreciation of yourself and others.

Applying a typing model can be an exceptionally valuable asset to team building and optimization. One of the critical challenges in working with teams is overcoming the conflicts of interest based on mischaracterization of team members. Such misconstrued perceptions can drain teams of precious energy as time is spent resolving conflict rather than attending to workloads and goals.

Good leaders are like conductors of an orchestra. The conductor knows the overall piece of music and all of the individual parts, but does not actually play an instrument. Instead, he provides the tempo, keeps all the musicians in balance, and allows each performer to contribute his best to the overall performance. Understanding his own style, he can communicate it to the orchestra to prepare them for how they will be asked to work together. Understanding other styles, he helps all the parts work together as a whole to accomplish something none of them could do alone.

DEVELOPMENTAL PERSPECTIVE

The Importance of Developmental Perspective

Developmental perspectives significantly influence how you see your role and function in the workplace, how you interact with others, and how you solve problems. The term "Developmental Perspective" can be described as "meaning making" or how you make sense of experiences. This is important because the algorithm you use to make sense of the world influences your thoughts and actions. Incorporating these perspectives as part of your interactions with others will improve your success as you lead a transformation effort.

> The term "Developmental Perspective" can be described as "meaning making" or how you make sense of experiences.

One of the characteristics of the Developmental Perspective model we believe is most important is that it lays out a natural and logical path for growth. While people move through these perspectives (levels) at different rates following a relatively predictable path, performance can be bolstered by understanding the needs at each perspective. Many adults will become more effective within their level without actually moving up a level or adding a perspective. Helping leaders move to later, more expansive (higher) developmental levels is also important to increasing organizational success. Development can be accelerated by creating an organizational culture that supports it. For this reason, by understanding the developmental process and perspectives, the pitfalls, and the enablers, you will be able to create an organization that supports development so that your leaders can effectively foster transformative efforts.

As an innovative leader, developing yourself isn't enough. You must also have an ability to understand others through the developmental lens and relate to them using Developmental Perspective as an important filter for interactions. This will inform the staffing selections you make, the roles you and others take within teams and groups, and the language and communication style you use when interacting with others in all settings. When working with Developmental Perspective, it is important to remember that we work with this concept so we can be more effective in our interaction with others. There are not better or worse levels; there are, however, better fits and worse fits. When making selections, we look at levels like we do skills. You are not selected for a job for which you do not have the appropriate skills. Instead, we add another criterion: Developmental Perspective. When selecting people for your change effort, it will be important to consider skills and match of Developmental Perspective to the role. We map Developmental Perspective to roles just as we map skills and make selections based on both criteria.

Because the concept of developmental perspectives is often overlooked in mainstream organizational literature and programs, and because we believe it is critical to effectively transforming organizations, we're intentionally giving it a lot of attention. We'll look at the six most common of those meaning-making approaches in greater detail; then, we will talk about how to use this concept when transforming your organization.

> When selecting people for your change effort, it will be important to consider skills and match of Developmental Perspective to the role.

In order to connect Developmental Perspective with Leader Type, let's look at how these models come together. While Leader Type is generally constant, you have the capacity to grow and develop your leadership perspective. In fact, leadership research strongly suggests that although inherent Leader Type determines your tendency to lead; good leaders develop over time. Therefore, it is often the case that leaders are perhaps both born and made. How leaders are made is best described using an approach that considers Developmental Perspective. Type remains consistent during your life while Developmental Perspective grows and is an important differentiator in leadership effectiveness.

This model helps us clarify how leaders develop individually and also applies to the organizational level to help select and train leaders more effectively. Here are some additional benefits of using a model of Developmental Perspective:

- It guides leaders in determining their personal development goals and action plans by helping leaders understand the next step in either enhancing their abilities at the current perspective or gaining access to the next perspective.

- It is a useful tool when determining which individuals and team members best fit specific roles considering skill and Developmental Perspective.

- It helps to identify which high-potential leaders to groom for growth opportunities.

- It can be used to create interview questions in the hiring process that illuminate key behaviors required for success in the job.

- It helps change agents understand the perspective of change targets and craft solutions that meet the needs of all stakeholders.

The Leadership Maturity Model and Developmental Levels/Perspectives

Figure 1.2 Maslow's Hierarchy of Needs

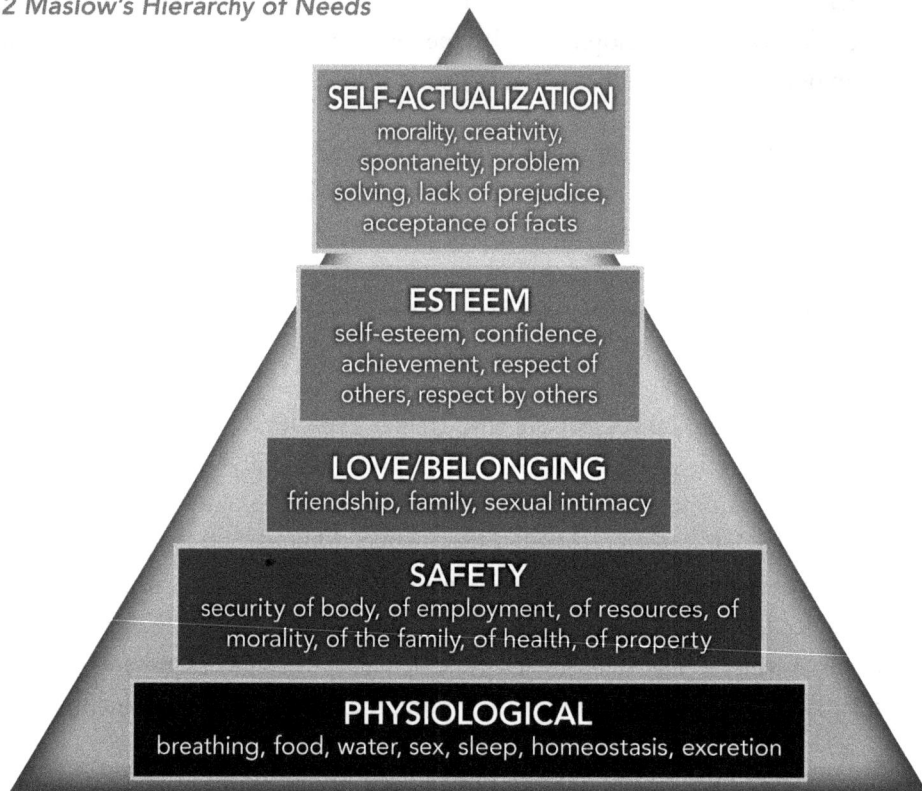

SELF-ACTUALIZATION
morality, creativity, spontaneity, problem solving, lack of prejudice, acceptance of facts

ESTEEM
self-esteem, confidence, achievement, respect of others, respect by others

LOVE/BELONGING
friendship, family, sexual intimacy

SAFETY
security of body, of employment, of resources, of morality, of the family, of health, of property

PHYSIOLOGICAL
breathing, food, water, sex, sleep, homeostasis, excretion

The Developmental Perspective approach is based on research and observation that, over time, people tend to grow and progress through a number of distinct stages of awareness and ability. One of the most well-known and tested developmental models is Abraham Maslow's *Hierarchy of Needs*—a pyramid visual aid Maslow created to help explain his theory of levels of human needs, both psychological and physical. As you ascend the steps of the pyramid, you can eventually reach a level of self-actualization.

Developmental growth occurs much like other capabilities grow in your life. Building on your Leader Type, you continue to grow, increasing access to or capacity for additional skills. We call this "transcend and include," in that you transcend the prior level, or perspective, and still maintain the ability to function at that perspective.

> People develop through stages at vastly differing rates, often influenced by significant events or "disorienting dilemmas."

Let us use the example of learning how to run to illustrate the process of development. You must first learn to stand and walk before you can run. And yet, as you eventually master running, you still effortlessly retain the earlier foundational skills that allowed you to stand and walk. In other words, you can develop your capacity to build beyond the basic skills you have now by moving through more progressive stages.

People develop through stages at vastly differing rates, often influenced by significant events or "disorienting dilemmas." Those events or dilemmas provide opportunities to begin experiencing your world from a completely different point-of-view. The nature of those influential events can vary greatly, ranging from positive social occasions like marriage, a new job, or the birth of a child, to negative experiences, such as job loss, an accident, or death of a loved one. These situations may often trigger more lasting changes in the way you think and feel. New developmental perspectives can develop gradually over time or, in some cases, transpire quite abruptly.

Some developmentally advanced people may be relatively young and yet others may experience little developmental growth over the course of a lifetime. Adding to the complexity of developmental growth is the fact that the unfolding of developmental perspectives is not predictably evident along the lines of age, gender, nationality, or affluence. We can only experientially sense indicators that help us identify Developmental Perspective when we listen and exchange ideas with others, employ introspection, and display openness to learning. In fact, most people naturally intuit and discern what motivates others as well as what causes some of their greatest challenges.

Developmental perspective is assessed by looking at three key factors:

- **Cognitive complexity** describes your capacity to take multiple perspectives and think through increasingly more complex problems. This is akin to solving an algebra problem with multiple variables. For example, a complex thinker is able to balance competing interests like employees' desire for higher pay, with customers' desire to pay low prices and receive good service.

- **Emotional competence** describes your self-awareness, self-management, awareness of others, and your ability to build and maintain effective relationships, along with your capacity for empathetic response.

- **Behavior** generally describes the actions you take.

A sense of time, or time horizon, is another essential feature in the development of perspective. For example, if a leader is limited by his Developmental Perspective to thinking about the completion of tasks within a timeline of three months or less, then optimally he should only be leading a part of the organization that requires short-term tasks. On the other hand, if a leader has the capacity to think and implement tasks with three-year time horizons, then that leader can and likely should be taking on a role that includes longer-term tasks. This could be a leader responsible for overseeing the implementation of an enterprise-wide computer system where the migration may take substantially more time and the process is more complex.

> Adding to the complexity of developmental growth is the fact that the unfolding of developmental perspectives is not predictably evident along the lines of age, gender, nationality, or affluence.

Elaborating on this example, there will be components of the team primarily responsible for the more tactical, hands-on part of the installation and who demonstrate shorter time horizon thinking. Obviously, they are held accountable for certain tasks within the plan but will not be responsible for designing the more strategic portions, nor be charged with the daily decisions that impact the overall budget.

Further still, imagine that one year into the program a key member of the team takes another job and the program manager (PM) becomes responsible for finding a suitable replacement. The program manager must consider all options when selecting a replacement. The most effective staffing solution for the program will need to account for potential changes over the next two years and how the replacement will impact overall program cost, quality of the final outcome, and team cohesiveness. Time horizons, along with developmental complexity, are directly applicable to innovative organizational decisions.

Detailed Review of Developmental Perspectives

In this section we'll examine the six developmental perspectives most often found in an organizational setting. We will also explore an example of a leader as she develops through some of those developmental perspectives while his underlying type remains unchanged. The following table reflects percentages of leaders testing at each perspective from the David Rooke and William R. Torbert article, "Seven Transformations of Leadership" in the Harvard Business Review. The details on developmental levels are derived from the work of Susanne Cook-Greuter.

Table 1.1

DESCRIPTION OF DEVELOPMENTAL LEVELS / PERSPECTIVES	% of Sample
Diplomat ■ Demonstrates predominately concrete thinking style ■ Hyper-concerned with social acceptance ■ Emphasis on conforming to the rules and norms of the desired group ■ Imagines that others think and feel the same as they do	12%
Expert ■ Demonstrates basic abstract thinking ■ Concerned with expressing a sense of individuality in sharp contrast to others ■ Concerned with measuring up to the "right" standards ■ Can often appear to be a perfectionist ■ Makes constant comparisons with others to gauge identity ■ Can often be critical and blame-oriented ■ Adept at developing multiple new solutions to problems but not able to determine the best fit solution ■ Can begin envisioning short-term time horizons: three months to one year	38%
Achiever ■ Basic ability to identify shades of grey and see conceptual complexity ■ Focuses on causes, achievement, and effectiveness ■ Considers others while pursuing their own individual agendas and ideas ■ Sees themselves as part of the larger group, yet separate and responsible for their own choices ■ Appreciates mutual expression of differences ■ Time horizon one to five years	30%

Individualist - Increased capacity for advanced complex thinking - Exhibits an ability to appreciate paradox in circumstances - Begins to value and use rudimentary aspects of intuition - Beginning awareness that perception shapes reality, including their own - Self-reflective and investigative of their own personalized assumptions, as well as those of others - Understands mutual interdependence with others - Lives personal convictions according to internal standards - Interest in feedback becomes important - Longer time horizon: five to ten years - Tend to move into change agent/consultant/portfolio roles	10%
Strategist - Perceives systematic patterns and long-term trends with uncanny clarity - Can easily differentiate objective versus subjective biased events - Exhibits a strong focus on self-development, self-actualization, and authenticity - Pursues actualizing personal convictions according to internal standards - Management style is tenacious, yet humble - Understands the importance of mutual interdependence with others - Integrating feedback into performance is important - Tend to move into change agent/consultant/portfolio roles - Well-advanced time horizon: approximately fifteen to twenty years with concern for legacy	4%
Magician/Alchemist - Seeks transformation of organizations not according to conventional goals but according to a higher order - Has a transforming ability to draw together opposites and initiate new directions from creative tension - Tends to build their own novel organizations or work on their own to offer their best contribution to humanity - Seen as visionary leaders - May lead from behind, or in a more subtle way - Time horizon in excess of twenty years	1%

Developmental Perspective and Organizational Effectiveness

Developmental perspective not only helps you as an individual leader create your growth path, it is also important in transforming your organization. The key to high performance is to align people and roles considering their Developmental Perspective. Different functions within the organization are best filled by people at different developmental perspectives. We call this their "fit" for the role, or more precisely, how the qualities associated with their Developmental Perspective align with requirements specific to the job. It is important for both leaders and organizations to support the health of all employees from a developmental standpoint and create an environment where each individual is in a role where he best fits and can move toward achieving his fullest potential.

> In order for you to be successful as a leader over the long run, it is essential to understand your proper "fit" within the organization—which includes understanding who you are and what you value, where you belong in the organization, and where you belong within the broader team and community stakeholders.

In order for you to be successful as a leader over the long run, it is essential to understand your proper "fit" within the organization—which includes understanding who you are and what you value, where you belong in the organization, and where you belong within the broader team and community stakeholders. If you find you are working in an environment that does not align with your Developmental Perspective, you may consider taking action. Actions could include finding an organization in which you are better aligned. If you are less developed than the organization, you may also want to make a concerted effort to develop. In a complex world, Developmental Perspective is only one of many variables to consider when selecting a job and when choosing to remain or move on. Since job change can be time consuming and difficult, we are not recommending changing because of this factor solely but rather raising it as a factor for consideration.

> Importantly, the goal is not merely to build an organization with all people at the "highest" Developmental Perspective, rather it is to select people for roles that allow them to function as effectively as possible individually and collectively.

It is also important to apply this concept to others as you are making hiring decisions, assigning people to roles, determining individual roles within a team, and communicating with others. Importantly, the goal is not merely to build an organization with all people at the "highest" Developmental Perspective, rather it is to select people for roles that allow them to function as effectively as possible individually and collectively. Your organization will be effective if it supports success for people at all levels and aligns them to roles that fit their capacity. Organizations that perceive one perspective as "better" will be less effective than organizations that leverage every perspective and design an organization where all levels can thrive concurrently and are working toward a collective goal of organizational success using a broad range of skills and perspectives.

You can use this developmental model with organizations in several ways:

- Make staffing and succession decisions using developmental perspectives. Considering Developmental Perspective along with past performance and technical and industry skills, align people to the roles that have the best "fit."

- Improve communication skills by applying a general understanding of Developmental Perspective to guide leaders in improving interpersonal effectiveness. Instead of simply communicating with others as ourselves, we recommend communicating with them based on their perspective. Understanding the perceptions of others from a developmental standpoint can dramatically improve interpersonal effectiveness. This is true with staff, peers, bosses, clients, family members, as well as other stakeholders.

- Improve management and leadership by applying an understanding of developmental perspectives allows a leader to clarify the needs of employees. For example, **Expert** employees want clear and specific directions and guidelines so they can do their tasks "right." **Individualists** want the freedom to determine the best approach to accomplishing tasks. Trying to manage these different developmental perspectives using the same approach will result in frustration and lost productivity.

- Comparing the organizational developmental level to your personal developmental level will help you better understand the organizational culture. Organizations develop along the same trajectory as people: they start with the need to establish basic rules and infrastructure, and then move to more complex functioning as they progress through the organizational lifecycle. Understanding the culture will help you because as an innovative leader you are continually aligning your intentions and behaviors with the culture and systems of the organization. While we do not address organizational maturity in this book, if you are interested in learning more, you may reference *Action Inquiry: The Secret of Timely and Transforming Leadership* by William R. Torbert included in the references section of this book.

Application

Dan is working as the general manager of an organization within a large government system. Dan's tests show him as a Strategist. His organization is experiencing major change because of political realignments after a scandal. His organization may transition from government operated to a nongovernmental agency in the near future in response to the realignment.

The following table gives a few examples of the challenges Dan faced with his team and solutions he developed as he became more familiar with how to apply his understanding of developmental perspectives. It is important to note that he did not "test" his staff but rather developed his own ability to generally evaluate them. This rough estimate gave him enough information to refine how he worked with people. I do want to be clear that you can only know the perspectives by doing a true assessment. For Dan's purposes, having a rough understanding gave him the information he needed to navigate the transformation he was implementing.

Dan acted in a manner that was highly ethical with this information. He did not use it to pigeon hole or marginalize people in any way. This assessment, like any other assessment tool that puts people into categories, can be used "against" or "for" people based on the criteria. We are talking about only using it to improve how we interact with people based on their perspective, not withholding promotions or marginalizing people in any way. We do not use it as a sole hiring tool although we do use our understanding of the criteria to develop interview questions that will help identify fit for the job based on Developmental Perspective.

The following table shows some of the challenges Dan faced, how these challenges can be seen through a developmental lens, and the solutions he devised based on his knowledge of developmental perspectives. He found this lens to be very helpful and it gave him a valuable tool to think through many of the challenges he had been facing over the past years.

Table 1.2

Challenge	Developmental Lesson	Solution
Asked people for input on large strategic issues and learned that many people on his staff really did not want to provide input. They wanted him to set the course and they would determine how to implement his plan within their individual departments	Many of his staff operate at the **Expert** level and, at that perspective, people want the boss to set the direction. The Expert might say something like: *How should I know how to proceed? That's what he's paid to figure out—not me.* Even worse, they could say: *If he doesn't know where we're going, then he's an incompetent boss and we should not follow him*	Realize that people at different levels will have different expectations about organizational roles. For a staff that is predominantly Expert, the leader needs to take a more active role in setting direction and ask for input at the **Task** level, not the **Strategic** level
Giving direction on organizational changes and job or task changes	His team members at the Individualist and Strategist levels want people to make suggestions about high level goals and step back to allow them to figure out how to accomplish the result His **Achievers** simply want to know the desired outcome and some general guidelines and measures—then they go to work. They want to know how they will be evaluated and who they are competing with so they could start the competition The **Experts** work better when told how to accomplish the task providing detailed steps to accomplish it. Because they want to do the job right, it is important to clarify what "right" looks like. In a transformation project this could look like very clearly defined operating procedures and "day in the life" scenarios	Understand the perspective of the people being asked to change and craft the materials accordingly. For jobs within the organization that primarily involve concrete tasks that have a "right and wrong" way to do them, it is important to provide clearly documented procedures and support materials so the employee can understand and perform well. Jobs that are more conceptual and are not generally defined by a clear right and wrong answer are usually performed by people with later level developmental perspectives and they respond best to general guidelines for the expected outcome rather than the step-by-step process about how to accomplish the assignment

Challenge	Developmental Lesson	Solution
Amount and type of information shared	His **Experts** are concerned with equity and fairness. To them, it is not fair if someone comes in late or leaves early when he is on vacation and not "watching them." They want the boss to be in charge and make decisions His **Achievers** are most concerned with accomplishing results and do not care so much about who is coming and going, or why, as long as they have what they need to accomplish their goals. They want quick answers so they can get back to the activities at hand and make things happen His **Individualists** are more concerned with involvement, inclusion, and ensuring that the broader community is being served by the mission. They want to reach consensus on issues that are important to them. This range of concerns and communication styles can make a simple staff meeting frustrating for everyone involved	Structure meetings using clear agendas and processes to accomplish the stated outcomes. If the goal is to share information that is not negotiable, structure the meeting accordingly If the meeting is to share status, send clear reports in advance and structure the meeting to share information that is important for the group to know. Only invite people who are impacted by the information and allow the balance of the group to focus on the results they are trying to accomplish. Collaboration and information sharing are often critical and can be very time consuming. Determine the most efficient approach given the culture and still focus on results If the meeting is to gain consensus on an important issue, build in time for conversation and clarify the process by which decisions will be reached (time box the conversation according to the importance of the issue)
Assign (hire) people to roles based on job related skills and also developmental level	People who perform well in individual contributor roles are often promoted to supervisory roles and they are ill equipped with the interpersonal skills to supervise and manage People with great skills in managing people to get things done are promoted to senior leadership roles and are often not inclined to slow down and consider longer-term implications and interconnection of consequences for their decisions People with great self-awareness and interpersonal skills are often promoted to executive roles and they may prefer inclusion and developing people over accomplishing the mission	When hiring for key roles, evaluate not only the job skills, but also the Developmental Perspective to successfully perform the role By expanding your hiring criteria, you can avoid some time consuming and costly pitfalls that adversely impact organizational health and success If you are interested in considering Developmental Perspective when hiring, you can create behavioral interview questions or scenarios that will test the thinking process and behavior of a leader in specific settings. While this will not tell you his Developmental Perspective, it will tell if he has access to the thinking and behavior you are seeking to be successful in the specific role

Our exploration of Developmental Perspective illustrates that having a deep understanding of perspectives is a critical element when transforming an organization. Understanding this element of leadership gives you a powerful tool to successfully implement transformation in response to adaptive challenges. It will help you identify and reduce the frustration, and increase employee engagement.

This section provided a brief introduction of a Developmental Perspective model and gives an example of how it can be applied. It is helpful for you to understand your own Developmental Perspective and also have a sense of the perspectives of those around you. You will want to have a sense of levels of key jobs or roles within the organization and use this understanding as input when designing your transformation initiative. It is important to note that you do not need precise scores, but often simply a general sense of people will help you quickly improve your effectiveness in working with them. Understanding how to apply this model effectively can greatly improve your communication effectiveness and interpersonal interactions with people who function at different perspectives.

RESILIENCE

We have now explored the qualities that comprise your Leader Type and the potential you have to enhance your Developmental Perspective. In examining Resilience, we further explore the physical and psychological nuances of both Leader Type and Developmental Perspective and how they impact individual and organizational well-being. The underlying premise is this: as a leader, you need to be physically and emotionally healthy to do a good job. In addition to physical and emotional health, the resilient leader also has a clear sense of life purpose and strong supportive relationships. Organizations need to consist of healthy people, and that happens when the leaders, culture, systems, and processes promote health during times of stress. For most people and organizations, enhancing Resilience requires a personal change. This personal focus on Resilience can be particularly difficult when working on a highly intense project that requires long hours and often travel. It is also important to creating highly effective project environments.

> Resilience can be viewed as the ability to adapt in the face of ongoing change while continuing to be both fluid in approach and driven toward attaining strategic goals.

There are two distinct ways to understand Resilience. First, from a leadership perspective, Resilience can be viewed as the ability to adapt in the face of ongoing change while continuing to be both fluid in approach and driven toward attaining strategic goals. Second, from a systems perspective, using an engineering analogy, Resilience is viewed as how much disturbance your systems can absorb before a breakdown. This view highlights the sturdiness of systems which could be something like a bridge or a larger system like an organizational system or environmental system. The first refers to fluidity and endurance while the second reflects stability. Addressing all aspects of Resilience is critical when transforming an organization.

The Importance of Resilience

Among the elements essential to leadership, Resilience is unique in that it integrates the physical and psychological aspects of Leader Type and Developmental Perspective to create the foundation of a leader's inner stability. This foundation enables you to demonstrate fluidity and endurance as you appropriately adapt to ongoing change. The lack of Resilience can put the health of individuals at risk and create a negative work environment that can ultimately impact the overall project effectiveness.

> The lack of resilience can put the health of individuals at risk and create a negative work environment that can ultimately impact the overall project effectiveness.

The Resilience Model

Figure 1.3 Elements of Resilience

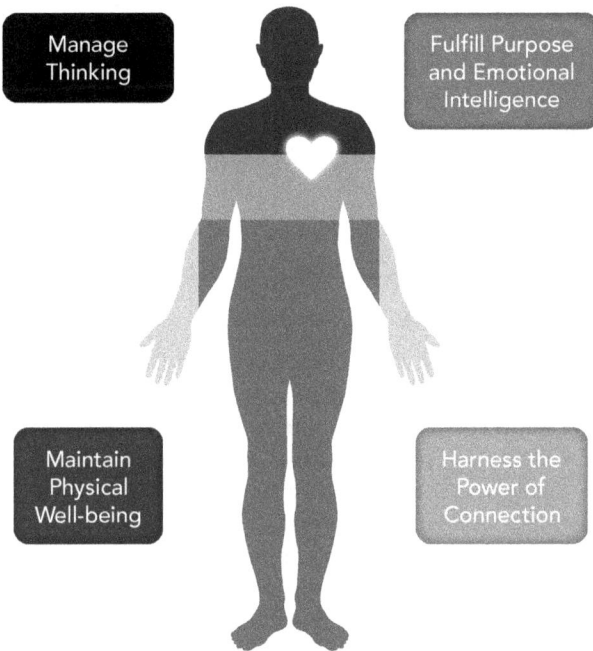

Manage Thinking

Fulfill Purpose and Emotional Intelligence

Maintain Physical Well-being

Harness the Power of Connection

Our Resilience approach is based on research by Dr. Suzanne Kobasa, as well as current business research from organizations such as Gallup that investigate well-being, and the Human Performance Institute that focuses on the corporate athlete.

Our model has four categories, shown in Figure 1.3. They are: maintain physical well-being, manage thinking, fulfill purpose using emotional intelligence, and harness the power of connection. These categories are interlinked and, consistent with leading research, must all be in balance to create long-term Resilience.

Leaders we work with often say they are too busy to take care of themselves. There is a balance between self-care and meeting all of our daily commitments. Most leaders fall short of their own personal Resilience goals and make daily choices for Resilience and personal health or against it. Our message here is that creating and maintaining Resilience is essential to your success. As you improve your Resilience, you will think more clearly and have a greater positive impact in your interactions with others; investing in your own Resilience supports the entire organization's effectiveness.

> As a leader transforming an organization, it is critical to attend to the leader behaviors that promote resilience as well as to the culture and organizational systems and processes.

As a leader transforming an organization, it is critical to attend to the leader behaviors that promote Resilience as well as to the culture and organizational systems and processes. To build a truly resilient organization, leaders must make deliberate choices about building this into key systems and processes as well as modeling behaviors that demonstrate the importance of Resilience. Most organizations in the United States do not sufficiently promote Resilience while many European companies, based on their culture and systems, have elements that promote building a resilient workforce. While we are interested in studying the variances between countries, this book does not provide additional examination.

Table 1.3 provides keys to building and retaining personal Resilience. For organizations to promote Resilience, they must support and reinforce these behaviors.

Table 1.3

KEYS TO BUILDING & RETAINING PERSONAL RESILIENCE

Maintain Physical Well-being	Fulfill Life Purpose
Are you getting enough: ■ Sleep ■ Exercise ■ Healthy food ■ Time in nature ■ Time to meditate and relax Are you limiting or eliminating: ■ Caffeine ■ Nicotine	Understand what you stand for. Maintain focus. Ask: ■ What is my purpose? ■ Why is it important to me? ■ What values do I hold that will enable me to accomplish my purpose? ■ What opportunities do I have in my professional life that help me to achieve my life purpose?
Manage Thoughts	**Harness the Power of Connection**
Practice telling yourself: ■ Challenges are normal and healthy for any individual or organization ■ My current problem is a doorway to an innovative solution ■ I feel inspired about the opportunity to create new possibilities that did not exist before	Practice effective communication: ■ Say things simply and clearly ■ Make communication safe by being responsive ■ Encourage people to ask questions and clarify if they do not understand your message ■ Balance advocacy for your point with inquiring about the other person's points ■ When you have a different point of view, seek to understand how and why the other person believes what they do in a non-threatening way ■ When in doubt, share information and emotions ■ Build trust by acting for the greater good

Resilience and Organizational Effectiveness

Organizations benefit significantly from having resilient leaders, and yet it is often organizational culture and systems that encourage behaviors at odds with Resilience. To bring about true individual and organizational change, leaders must incorporate Resilience into the larger picture of leadership development and organizational effectiveness.

As an innovative leader, you will develop action plans for transitioning your organization from the status quo to one that supports resilient leaders and workers. As an example, an innovative leader we worked with committed to encouraging employees to negotiate due dates for non-critical tasks. In this case, employees previously had not taken personal time off because they felt the need to be "on call" continually even when their tasks did not require this level of availability. Having due dates that appropriately address the criticality of tasks allowed them the flexibility to integrate time for exercise and better work-life balance that resulted in feeling more energetic and engaged when on the job. By focusing on changing systems and processes, as well as promoting a culture that supports a combination of organizational results balanced with Resilience, people within the organization will have the capacity necessary to navigate organizational changes without being overwhelmed unnecessary.

> To bring about true individual and organizational change, leaders must incorporate resilience into the larger picture of leadership development and organizational effectiveness.

Having the ability to maintain physical well-being, manage thoughts, fulfill purpose using emotional intelligence, and harness the power of connection during times of transition is critical to successfully transforming organizations.

SITUATIONAL ANALYSIS

While we have focused heavily thus far on building individual capacity for leaders and employees, understanding the organization's background or context is equally important. Consider that your experience isn't merely a collection of events and random happenstance; rather, it is fundamentally shaped by the background interplay of your individual attributes, shared relationships, and involved institutions.

The Importance of Situational Analysis

The nature of human experience is more than simple personal expression. Every moment of experience is influenced by a mutual interaction of intention, action, culture, and systems. All four of these basic dimensions are fundamental to every experience we have and mutually shape them in all circumstances. Situational analysis employs the four-dimensional view of reality to balance in the most comprehensive way possible the situations you face. We refer to these four qualities as intention (self), action, culture, and systems. This balance—without favoring elements—is critical to effectively transform your organization.

> Situational Analysis employs the four-dimensional view of reality to balance in the most comprehensive way possible the situations you face. We refer to these four qualities as intention (self), action, culture, and systems. This balance—without favoring elements—is critical to effectively transform your organization.

A multi-faceted approach provides a more complete and accurate view of events and situations than our traditional approach that often favors analysis based primarily on a systems or process view and excludes culture and leadership impact. Leaders often take a partial approach to changing organizations. They overemphasize system's change with little or no consideration to the culture or how their personal views and actions shape the content and success of the change. Situational analysis enables you to create alignment across the four dimensions on an ongoing basis.

Integral Model and Situational Awareness

Figure 1.4 Integral Model

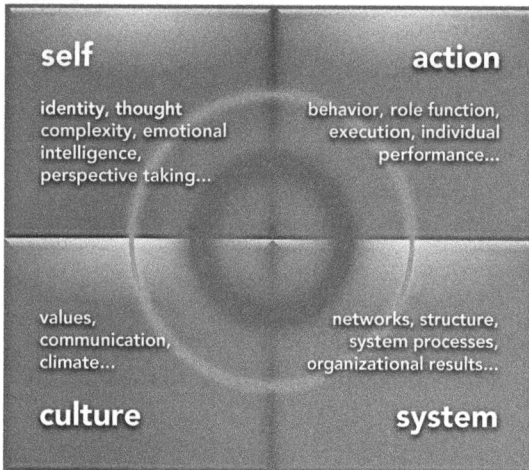

self
identity, thought complexity, emotional intelligence, perspective taking...

action
behavior, role function, execution, individual performance...

culture
values, communication, climate...

system
networks, structure, system processes, organizational results...

American-born philosopher Ken Wilber developed a conceptual scheme to illustrate the four basic dimensions of being that form the backbone of experience. His Integral Model provides a map that shows the mutual relationship and interconnection among four dimensions, in which each represents the basic elements of human experience.

When using Situational Analysis, you are cultivating simultaneous awareness of all four dimensions. Let's look at an example. This is a sample narrative taken from Integral Life Practice (Wilber et al) that will give you a more experiential description of how these dimensions shape every situation in your life.

Example: *"Visualize yourself kicking off a major change initiative that will have significant impact on the way the organization uses data going forward:*

Self *(Upper-Left Quadrant, "I"):* You feel excited and a little nervous about the big program kick-off meeting today. Thoughts race through your head about how this will impact the overall strategy to approaching a key market.

Culture *(Lower-Left Quadrant, "We"):* You enter a familiar culture of shared meaning, values, and expectations that are communicated, explicitly and implicitly, every day. You understand how things work and also understand that this program could have a significant impact that will change the organization's norms in many ways.

Action *(Upper-Right, "It"):* Your physical behaviors are obvious: walking, waving good morning, opening a door, sitting down at your desk, turning on the computer, and so on. Brain activity, heart rate, and perspiration all increase as the important meeting draws nearer. You are preparing to kick off the meeting with a motivational presentation about the importance of this program on the organization's ability to meet key performance goals over the next five years. This program will be a game changer for your organization and its success depends in part on your ability to manage it successfully.

System *(Lower-Right, "Its"):* Elevators, powered by electricity generated miles away, lift you to your floor. You easily navigate the familiar environment, arrive at your desk, and log on to the organization's intranet to check the latest global updates on the enterprise software system. You are familiar with the tracking software that will allow you to manage this complex program as well as the project management processes you will use to run the program. You are also aware that several systems and processes will change as a result of your program, and you will be responsible for ensuring that change is efficient and effective.

A crucial part of transforming your organization is leveraging your capacity as an innovative leader to be aware of the four dimensions at any given moment and to identify alignments and misalignments. Even though you cannot physically see the values, beliefs, and emotions that strongly influence the way an individual colleague perceives himself and the world, nor a group's culture, emotional climate or collective perception, they still profoundly shape the vision and potential of leaders to address adaptive problems and transform the organization.

The Importance of Alignment and Influence in Organizational Effectiveness

We use an alignment model to describe how using Situational Analysis as a tool allows you not only to make more informed decisions, but also helps you optimize performance within yourself, your teams, and the broader organization. Alignment of all dimensions is the key to optimizing performance.

Building alignment across the four dimensions starts with self, culture, action and systems, and examines how these dimensions create an aligned system that is cohesive and integrated. Figure 1.5 shows the image of an aligned system and the following section describes how the dimensions are aligned.

> A crucial part of transforming your organization is leveraging your capacity as an innovative leader to be aware of the four dimensions at any given moment and to identify alignments and misalignments.

Figure 1.5 Alignments across Dimensions

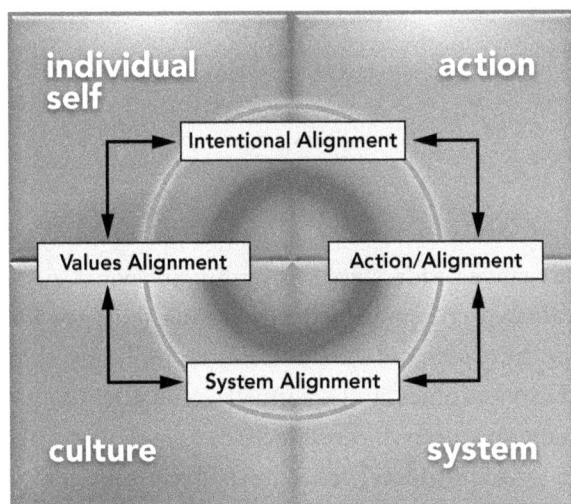

- **Personal Alignment:** the ongoing process of coordinating your self-dimension (intentions, identify, thoughts, emotional intelligence, and perspective taking) with your action dimension (behavior, role function, execution, and individual performance) to create a sense of personal integrity within yourself and inspire trust in others.

- **Action Alignment:** the ongoing process of coordinating your action-dimension (behavior, role function, execution, and individual performance) with the organization's system-dimension (network, structure, system processes, and organizational results) to create recognition for you and efficient and effective organizational results.

- **System Alignment:** the ongoing process of coordinating system-dimension (network, structure, system processes, and organizational results) with the culture-dimension (organizational values, communication, and climate) to increase functional efficiency among organizational culture and systems.

■ **Values Alignment:** the ongoing process of coordinating the culture-dimension (organizational values, communication, and climate) with the self-dimension (intentions, identify, thoughts, emotional intelligence, and perspective taking) to create a sense of individual alignment with organizational values that cause individuals to feel they "fit" in the organization and that the organization has a sense of value-based leaders.

While we have not drawn the arrows on the diagonal, when the dimensions are aligned as shown in Figure 1.5, all dimensions reflect balanced alignment. This alignment is important because it minimizes confusion and productivity loss. When misaligned, employees are often given conflicting direction or told to act in one way and then penalized during the appraisal process because different behaviors are rewarded rather than behaviors they were told about.

Increased Situational Analysis helps you create holistic solutions by removing misalignment among the four key dimensions. The process of deliberately evaluating the four basic dimensions of any experience can provide you with a tool to identify potential disconnects that could waste resources and cause great frustration for you and your employees. From a leadership perspective this will allow you to have greater impact because you have taken the deliberate step to align all the dimensions.

> The process of deliberately evaluating the four basic dimensions of any experience can provide you with a tool to identify potential disconnects that could waste resources and cause great frustration for you and your employees.

The goal is to align the four dimensions through deliberate understanding of the dimensions and the interconnections across each one. Deliberately focusing on alignment is a key lever to implementing innovative changes that allow your organization to thrive.

LEADERSHIP BEHAVIORS

Let's now explore the fifth and final dimension of Innovative Leadership: Leadership Behaviors. As we shift our focus to the more actionable craft of leadership as defined by behaviors and skills, we will examine the impact of observable leadership skills for the leader and the leadership team. Leadership skills, as well as hard skills, are critical to success and serve as objective performance measures of Innovative Leadership. Hard skills fall into two primary categories: industry-related knowledge, skills, and aptitudes; and functional knowledge, skills, and aptitudes. Leadership behaviors are the result of knowledge, skills, and aptitudes specifically related to the craft of leadership. We will be using the term Leadership Behaviors in this workbook when referring to leadership knowledge, skills, and aptitudes and the resulting behaviors. Both hard skills and Leadership Behaviors are critical to successful organizational transformation. The balance between the importance of hard skills and Leadership Behaviors will shift as the leader progresses in the organization and as leadership skills and behaviors become increasingly important with career advancement and with complex roles involving the implementation of organizational transformation.

Leadership behaviors are important because they are the objective actions the leader takes that transform the organization. We have all seen brilliant leaders behave in a manner that damages their organization, and we have seen other leaders consistently behave in ways that promote ongoing organizational success. Effective leadership behavior drives organizational success and, conversely, ineffective Leadership Behaviors drive organizational dysfunction or failure. In this chapter, we will look at the Leadership Behaviors associated with Innovative Leadership and successful organizational transformation for both individual leaders and leadership teams. An example is the leader who seeks to include others in decisions where their expertise will enhance the outcome then shares credit, versus the leader who rushes through decisions and misses key input causing others to correct the oversights while trying to ensure the leader saves face.

An example of the need for both hard skills and Leadership Behaviors is in the role Chief Data Officer (CDO). To be successful, this CDO must possess the hard skills in data organization and analysis and the Leadership Behaviors to effectively lead. If either of these sets of skills is missing, the leader and the organization are at risk of underperforming. Early in his career, a mastery of data analytics set him apart from his peers. As he progressed into the senior leadership ranks and ultimately to the role of CDO, his use of Leadership Behaviors became his primary focus while he continued to need hard skills and expertise in analytics. Others may have followed a different career path where they developed skills in financial analysis, business analytics, or statistics. There are many paths to build these skills, the important distinction to remember is a leader will need both technical skills and also specific leadership skills.

> Effective leadership behavior drives organizational success and, conversely, ineffective Leadership Behaviors drive organizational dysfunction or failure.

One area we have not yet discussed is that of making decisions about who is on the leadership team and who is not. These decisions involve promotion, and they also involve decisions to move people into new roles and possibly out of the company. The following section is about Leadership Behaviors from a self-development perspective. As a leader, what behaviors support the organization's success, and which ones do not?

There are several different ways to discuss leadership from a skills perspective:

There are several strengths in conceptualizing leadership from a skills [actions] perspective. First, it is a leader-centered model that stresses the importance of the leader's abilities, and it places learning skills at the center of effective leadership performance. Second, the skills approach describes leadership in such a way that it makes it available to everyone. Skills are behaviors that we all can learn to develop and improve. Third, the skills approach provides a sophisticated map that explains how effective leadership performance can be achieved.

—Peter G. Northouse,
Leadership Theory and Practice, February 2012

Leadership Competency Model

The integrated, measurable, role-specific approach associated with leadership competency models has several advantages. While there are several effective leadership competency approaches, current competency models that measure and develop leadership knowledge, skills, abilities, and behaviors (KSABs) often occur both too late in the leadership development process and are too tactical in nature.

> Arising from the research on leadership developmental framework, these Action-Logic competencies serve as the roadmap for the planning, benchmarking, and measurement of effective transformational leaders.

As significant, the KSABs required to be an effective leader or manager only tangentially address the development of effective executive leadership and transformational skills. A mounting dossier of research points to developmental maturity as the key to effective leadership, especially as it relates to transformational leadership abilities. Researchers such as Ken Wilber, Susanne R. Cook-Greuter, Bill Torbert, and Terri O'Fallon define stages of developmental growth, which they call Action-Logics (AL). These action logics are also the foundation for the developmental perspectives. They have transformed these ALs into a leadership development framework with measurable stages. The noteworthy difference between these ALs versus traditional KSABs is that ALs help define the leader's developmental lens rather than the leader's learned information. This is analogous to the difference between a competency that defines the use of a tool and a competency that defines the use of the hand using the tool. ALs have broader implications. We believe the ALs are an important foundation for the transformation activities described throughout this workbook. While traditional KSABs like Executive Communication Skills and Situational Awareness tend to break down under conditions of stress and uncertainty, ALs tend to hold true under stress. This is due to how they define who the developed person has become rather than what behaviors the person has learned to execute. Ultimately, both are critical for effective physician leadership.

The table below details seven transformational AL Leadership Competencies. Arising from the research on leadership developmental framework, these Action-Logic competencies serve as the roadmap for the planning, benchmarking, and measurement of effective transformational leaders. Each of the seven developmental competencies is measurable and can be effectively used to facilitate developmental growth.

Table 1.4

Transformational Leader Action-Logics Competencies At Strategist And Beyond	
This is a list of "Level 5" competencies focused on how you make sense of the world. The way you see the world drives how you behave. Few people operate fully at this level; we are providing this list to help you see what Level 5 Leaders generally experience when they are operating at their highest potential.	
Professionally humble	**Cares about getting it right ahead of being right** ■ Committed to personal and organizational mission as "North Star" and focal point for where to invest energy in service of leaving a legacy ■ Cares more about the organization and the result than her/ his image ■ Freely, happily, and instinctively gives credit to others ■ Puts principles ahead of personal gain

Dogmatically committed to right action	**Is unstoppable and unflappable when on a mission** - Has the dichotomous ability to be fully committed, hard driving, fully focused, and yet not experienced as either myopic or stubborn - Has the ability to 'stay the course' when under pressure
A 360 degree thinker	**Has the 'balcony view' of the business** - Innately understand the systems, constraints, perceptions, near term, long term, and secondary impacts of business strategy and decisions, and how to transform them to complete amazing results - Balances competing commitments of multiple constituents on a regular basis - Thinks in terms of systems, dialogues, and transformations when focusing on constraints and perceptions—consider the organizational context when making recommendations - Strong commitment to continual personal learning and building learning systems - Understands cross organizational impact—striving to understand the interconnection across multiple complex systems and make highly informed decisions considering implications across broader contexts
Intellectually versatile	**Has developed interests, expertise, and curiosity beyond the job and organization** - Despite a devout commitment to the job and the organization, they are always interested and involved with areas beyond their comfort zones - Takes a special interest in political, national, and international developments - Use external interest to enhance legacy and provide balance in life
Highly authentic and reflective	**Is not constrained by personal appearance but is highly focused on personal behavior** - Highly committed to personal growth and development, and growing and developing others - Is so undefended and open to feedback it may be surprising - Seeks out discussions and feedback even in uncomfortable situations - Able to manage emotions in the most difficult situations—understand the impact and contagious nature of emotions so they develop skills to recognize them, manage/metabolize them, and relate to others productively - Able to maintain perspective in times of stress, taking a long-term view and remaining vision focused, they are less challenged by difficult situations than others - Demonstrates emotional courage—willing to confront challenging situations - Continually looking for ways to enable the organization to improve its ability to meet its mission more efficiently and effectively

Able to inspire followership	**Has the special ability to connect with people at all levels of the organization to create a shared vision**
	▪ Intuitively understands change, the steps to managing change, and how to help the organization overcome its resistance to change
	▪ Has an innate ability to diffuse conflict without avoiding or sidestepping the source of the conflict
	▪ Has a great ability to use humor effectively to put people at ease
	▪ Able to relate to a broad range of people and understand their motivators and stressors
	▪ Innately connect projects to the individual goals while working to overcome barriers
	▪ Able to provide valuable feedback to others in a manner that is supportive of growth and development of the recipient
Innately collaborative	**Welcomes collaboration in a quest for novel solutions that serve the highest outcome for all involved**
	▪ Seeks input from multiple perspectives—valuing diverse points of view
	▪ Creates solutions to complex problems by creating new approaches that did not exist, pulling together constituents in novel ways, creating broader and more creative alliances
	▪ Understands that in a time of extreme change, input from multiple stakeholders with diverse points of view are required

Leadership Behaviors and Organizational Effectiveness

Effective leadership mindsets and behaviors drive effective organizations. As we build on the Situational Analysis model, effective leaders' behaviors—also referred to as "actions" in the Situational Analysis model—are one of the four dimensions (upper right quadrant of Figure 1.4). If these effective behaviors or actions are aligned with the other dimensions, then the whole system is affected by who the leader is and how the leader behaves. According to the alignment component of the Situational Analysis model, effective leaders align self (AL competencies) and actions to create personal alignment; they align self and cultures to create values alignment; they align their actions and systems to create action alignment; and they align cultures and systems to create system alignment. If the leader's behaviors or actions are ineffective, the entire system will be ineffective. If his behaviors are ineffective and the system is not aligned, he will still cause organizational dysfunction. If, on the other hand, the leader is behaving in a manner that supports the organization and creates alignment across the dimensions, the entire organization will benefit.

> Understanding the behaviors associated with Innovative Leadership creates the foundation for you to examine your own behavior and determine where you are functioning as an innovative leader and where you would like to make changes.

Leadership behaviors are objective and measurable actions. Understanding the behaviors associated with Innovative Leadership creates the foundation for you to examine your own behavior and determine where you are functioning as an innovative leader and where you would like to make changes. It also supports you in aggregating individual scores to develop a team profile, understanding your greatest strengths and risks. This increased understanding can help you not only identify areas of improvement, but can also leverage the strengths you already have across the team that may not have been fully visible prior to the assessment.

REFLECTION QUESTIONS

Following is a list of questions designed to help you start thinking about how this content will apply to your immediate work.

How can you use a type-based approach to guide how you interact with others?

Would an increased use of type knowledge help improve your team effectiveness by promoting discussion among team members about preferred roles and communication styles?

How can you use this exploration of Developmental Perspective shape how you work with different groups of people during your transformation effort?

How can you include your understanding of Developmental Perspective into your hiring decisions by mapping Developmental Perspective or fit for role to each key role?

Where would you rank your resilience in each of the four categories?

How can you promote team resilience within your culture and systems while you transform the organization?

How do you, as a leader, model resilient behavior that is visible to others and sets the tone for your belief that resilience is important for your success and the success of your people?

Where do you see misalignments between what you value and how you act because of pressures from your organization?

REFLECTION QUESTIONS (CONT.)

Where do you see misalignments between what your organization says it values and the systems it has put in place, such as performance management and compensation?

▰▰▰▰▰▰▰

As you are implementing change, how will you use Situational Analysis to ensure that all dimensions are addressed and aligned?

▰▰▰▰▰▰▰

If you were to receive feedback on your leadership competencies, where would you excel? Where would you fall short?

▰▰▰▰▰▰▰

Do your Leadership Behaviors match the requirements of your job? Do you require new skills to support leading an analytics transformation effort?

▰▰▰▰▰▰▰

How do you use your understanding of Leadership Behaviors to increase your team effectiveness?

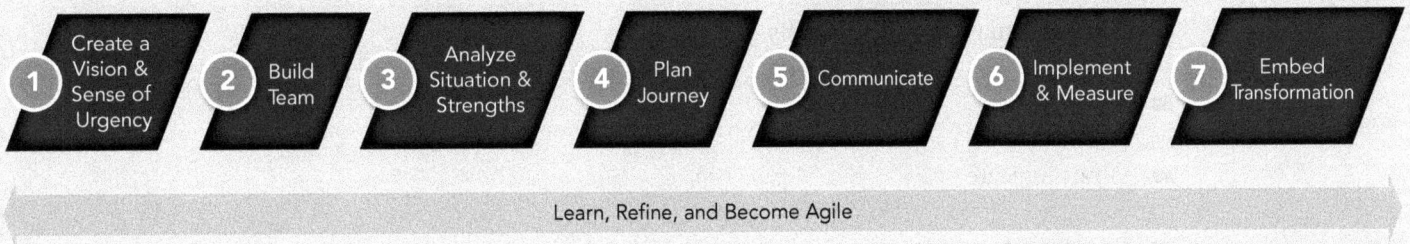

| 1 | Create a Vision & Sense of Urgency | 2 | Build Team | 3 | Analyze Situation & Strengths | 4 | Plan Journey | 5 | Communicate | 6 | Implement & Measure | 7 | Embed Transformation |

Learn, Refine, and Become Agile

SECTION II

Using Innovative Leadership - The Art of Analytics Transformation

In Chapter One, we defined and explained the five key elements of Innovative Leadership, leaders and leadership teams used to create a foundation for implementing organizational transformation. Now you're ready for Chapters Two through Eight: The Art of Leading Organizational Transformation. This is the interactive section of the workbook containing exercises, worksheets, reflection questions, and examples. It is designed to provide a step-by-step process to support you in successfully leading your organizational transformation. This book has been tested with clients, as well as hundreds of working adults participating in an MBA program. It has been tested and revised over five years to create a process that makes a high impact on leaders' capacity to transform organizations.

The process steps are:

- Create a vision and sense of urgency

- Recruit and build your team

- Analyze situation and strengths

- Plan journey

- Communicate

- Implement and measure

- Embed transformation

While this model appears to be linear, it can be used sequentially with overlapping steps, or the concepts and tasks can be applied in an Agile manner. The sequential approach will provide a logical foundation that will continue to grow throughout the process. For organizations that have adopted Agile methodologies, this model includes many techniques and templates that will help your enterprise increase commitment and adopt the analytic models your teams create.

> While this model appears to be linear, it can be used sequentially with overlapping steps, or the concepts and tasks can be applied in an Agile manner.

The comprehensiveness of these exercises coupled with reflection exercises will give you the necessary insight into yourself and your organization to lead your organizational transformation. We have found that when leaders work through these steps sequentially, they often return to earlier stages of the process to clarify and sometimes change details they had originally thought were correct. The structure of our process will continue to challenge you to refine the work you have accomplished in prior tasks. First ideas are often good ones, but when you work through the process and build on your knowledge, you will often find you will benefit from returning to earlier steps and refining your information.

The time you spend with this workbook is an investment in your development and your organization's analytics transformation success. Leading a transformative effort requires reflection and thorough evaluation of both yourself and the organization. This reflection will take time and is critical to your success. We strongly encourage you to engage in the process with as much time and attention as possible. The value you ultimately take from this process is closely linked to the time you invest.

CHAPTER 2
CREATE A VISION AND SENSE OF URGENCY

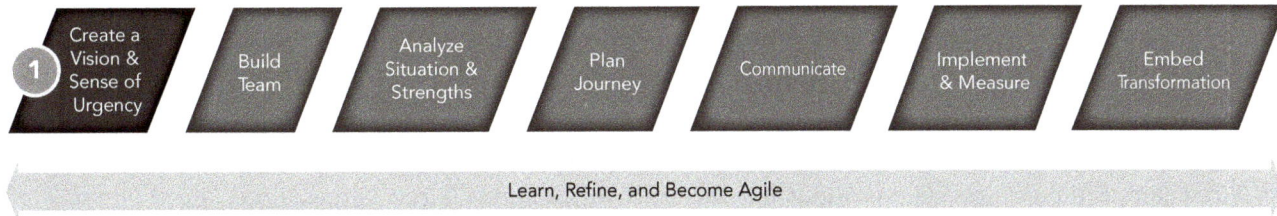

Create a Vision & Sense of Urgency	Build Team	Analyze Situation & Strengths	Plan Journey	Communicate	Implement & Measure	Embed Transformation

Learn, Refine, and Become Agile

The first stage of successful analytics program implementation and associated business transformation is to ensure that key stakeholders understand the vision of the transformation, the guiding principles, and why the change is urgent and necessary. Along with defining the reason for the program, it is important for the leaders who are chartering the program to clearly convey what they expect the organization to accomplish, who will accomplish it, and how success will be measured.

This vision and sense of urgency generally begin at the top of the organization or business unit with those who charter or authorize the change. They must be aligned with the overall organizational vision and guiding principles (or the principles that the organization is using moving toward) and move the organization toward accomplishing strategic objectives.

> The leadership team clarifies the vision, goals, and business value for the change.

While leaders charter the change, often employees have known for some time that a change is needed and many are willing and able to participate and champion the movement from inside the organization. Many of these supportive employees will volunteer to work on the program in varying capacities.

The outcomes of this phase are that leaders and key stakeholders have a clear understanding of the foundation for the change that aligns the program with the overall organizational strategy, and a program charter that empowers a specific set of leaders and employees to embark on the change program.

Tools

The first task is to decide what should be transformed to enable the organization to meet its strategic objectives. The leadership team clarifies the vision, goals, and business value for the change. During this process, they also look at the cost involved by not implementing the program. Because leading a transformational change in a business can constitute a "big bet," it is imperative that the leaders involved both have a clear understanding of why they are embarking on the change and look at ways to test their thinking by making small incremental changes along the way to validate their decisions. While this seems complicated, most businesses do not fail because they failed at making a small change but rather, they wagered and discovered that either the bet was wrong or the business environment changed along the way, and the direction they were taking was no longer the one they should have taken. For these reasons, it is important to look at how to manage the risk associated with organizational transformation including analytics programs.

For a program like we will see in the case study, the steering committee decided to implement in phases and one site at a time. We will read more about those decisions in the case study. In many cases, you will find organizations using Agile processes to speed up and get more value out of IT projects. If you have not used an Agile approach, it is an approach to project management that is typically used in software development. It helps teams respond to the unpredictability of building software through incremental, iterative work cadences known as "sprints." according to www.agilemethodology.org. Agile processes are based on iterative and incremental development methodologies. As the scale grows, the administration of Agile teams must also scale. The Scaled Agile Framework as referenced at www.scaledagileframework.com is an excellent information source if you need guidance. Project implementations can be Agile, Waterfall (traditional sequential design approach), or a combination. While the Agile methods are not required, they are generally more appropriate and successful for analytic initiatives.

One of the tools we like to use to help determine which program to take on to meet the strategic goals is the Change Foundation Assessment. It is likely that you, as part of the leadership team, will evaluate many potential change programs using several of these assessments, and the organization will rank the various programs and determine which ones to take on and how they are time-phased to provide the greatest benefit at the least cost and disruption to the organization.

Change Foundation Assessment

Objective: The foundation assessment is designed to help you understand and clearly articulate why this program is happening and serves as the basis for next steps in data collection. In addition, the analysis begins to build the foundation for the charter and the information that will be communicated in the awareness packages to new program team members and change network (people who support the program on a part-time or ad-hoc basis). As you explore which possible changes will help you accomplish your vision, it will be important to revisit the idea of adaptive challenges presented in the introduction, remembering that adaptive challenges require concurrent changes to all four dimensions of the system, the leader's intentions and behaviors, along with the organization's culture and systems. It will be important to take this into account when defining the change and the change foundation. Because analytics programs often involve significant change in the way the leader and the organization think about their business, these are often considered adaptive changes.

Table 2.1

Change Foundation Assessment – Key Components

Data sources: May include latest company strategy documents/presentations, research reports, management meeting presentation slides, white papers, etc.

Organizational vision: The organization's fundamental, enduring reason for being; a clear articulation of why the organization exists

Strategic goals: Which part(s) of the organizational strategy does this program support?

Program objectives: Describe what the program will accomplish, or the business value it will deliver, and how success will be measured

Key stakeholders: Describe key stakeholders understanding of the change initiative's objectives and how they fully support the organizational change required/sought

Diagnostic activities: What analysis has been used to evaluate the program and confirm the situation?

Expected changes: Aspects of the present state that will have to change?

Consequences: What happens if changes are not implemented?

Approvals: Who authorized the program?

Program motivations: What are the motivations to pursue a different state from what it is currently?

Implementation activities: What are the high level activities required for successful implementation?

Processes in scope: What processes will be impacted by the change?

Resources: Considerations should include sufficient and available work force, budget, and competencies to ensure successful transformation

Risk management: How can the program be broken into phases to manage investment and risk?

Sponsors: Who are the individuals or groups who have the power to sanction or legitimize change? If there are multiple sponsors, they will likely include representation from across the organization

Measurable outcomes: What specific changes or results will the organization use to evaluate program success?

After programs have been evaluated and selected for implementation, it is time to create a program charter for each of the selected programs.

Program Charter

Objective: Formal document is designed to establish the program and clarify program goals (what is expected) at a high level and how it will be accomplished (guiding principles, assumptions, and constraints). The charter will include information you identify in the reflection questions.

You'll find that you have already gathered much of the information in the assessment phase you need for your charter. You'll take the information from the programs determined to have met the requirements as full scale programs and add the additional information needed to charter a team. You may find you enhance the information from the assessment phase depending on your specific situation and approach.

Creating the charter overlaps with the second step in the process: build your team. We will go into greater detail about who to select and how to structure the team in the next chapter as well as how to engage participants. It will be important to consider the program structure as you create the charter.

"Although traditional hierarchies and processes—which together form a company's 'operating system'—are optimized for day-to-day business, they can't handle the challenges of mounting complexity and rapid change. The solution is a second operating system, devoted to the design and implementation of strategy that uses an Agile, network-like structure and a different set of processes. The new operating system continually assesses the business, the industry, and the organization, and reacts with greater agility, speed, and creativity than the existing one. It complements rather than overburdens the hierarchy, thus freeing the latter to do what it's optimized to do. It actually makes enterprises easier to run and accelerates strategic change."

—John P. Kotter,
"Accelerate," *Harvard Business Review*, November 2012

We agree with this premise for many initiatives—especially those that are addressing adaptive challenges. In these cases, the hierarchy may preclude the team from developing solutions that are sufficiently comprehensive. If your program will operate outside of the traditional hierarchy, it will be important to spell that out in the charter and also to select people who have the capacity to work in an Agile environment that, in some cases, functions more like a network than a hierarchy. This is where we build on the Innovative Leadership framework. Leaders with the ability to function at a higher Developmental Perspective will be more effective in this alternate operating system than those who have a center of gravity at achiever or earlier levels. We will continue to explore team selection in the next chapter.

If you are implementing a series of interconnected projects like those referenced in this example, you may want to create a network structure where multiple projects are managed collectively. In traditional program management terms there are multiple projects that combine to form a program. This may still be the case, but the management structure may be less traditionally hierarchical and more fluid, using more Agile governing approaches.

For analytic programs, we recommend using the Agile method for the implementation. When the initial vision is established, key features or functional areas can be prioritized based on business value, data quality and availability, model maturity, and technical prerequisites. By setting the priorities at a more granular level, each component can be developed individually and deployed as soon as the product owner has validated the value for that feature. In an analytic solution, there are many prerequisites. The product owner can weigh those relative to the needs for immediate gains. By remaining flexible and responsive, the entire team will be able to drive a faster transformation for the organization.

One additional approach is called Holacracy, a comprehensive practice for structuring, governing, and running an organization. It replaces today's top-down predict-and-control paradigm with a new way of distributing power and achieving control. It is a new "operating system" that instills rapid evolution in the core processes of an organization. While it is beyond the scope of this book, we mention it here to let you know that there are well-tested approaches to governance that are designed for Agile, networked environments, and structures. More information can be found at www.holacracy.org.

> For analytic programs, we recommend using the Agile method for the implementation.

A traditional charter will include the following sections and may be modified to meet your specific program requirements:

Table 2.2

Project Charter – Template	
1. Business problem statement	
2. Vision and objectives	
3. Success criteria	
4. Scope	
5. Timeline and deliverables	
6. Assumptions and constraints	
7. Interconnected programs	
8. Risks	
9. Communication strategy	
10. Change management plan	
11. Team	
12. Charter approval signatures	

Stories and Examples

In the next section, we will provide an example of how these tools have been used. George is a composite drawn from our experience with several clients. We will share the case study throughout the balance of the book to give you a realistic flavor of how each of these tools is used to support a transformation effort. George will complete each step in the process so you can see how tools and reflection questions are used to support transformation.

Sample Responses for George as a Strategist

In Chapter One, we talked about Developmental Perspective. We did not go into great detail in this section, but referred to leaders who were highly developed on the Maslow hierarchy. We will discuss the tools that measure this development in Chapter Four. For the purpose of our introduction, we would like to point out that George tests highly developed on the Developmental Perspective scale. George has a strong ability to successfully lead complex change efforts. We believe it is helpful for you to read how someone with this perspective (referred to as strategist throughout this book) would look at this change effort, so George will be responding to reflection questions from the strategist Developmental Perspective. Through our client work and teaching, we've found that giving examples of how each perspective uses these exercises to be especially insightful in the personal growth process. We have tried to capture George's internal thought process in these exercises in a way that is rare in a business context, but helpful for the purpose of professional development and leading organizational transformation.

Introduction to George

At age 45, George recently joined a global firm as the Chief Data Officer (CDO). On a daily basis, he is involved in transforming the organization across multiple locations around the world. When he took the job, the organization had several computer systems and used Excel spreadsheets extensively. Through his analysis, he determined that implementing an analytics-driven tool for pricing and delivery would both decrease the enterprise operating expense and improve margins through optimized pricing. He partnered with his colleagues in the business units to confirm the potential value of the effort, as well as the degree of change required. They realized that new technologies would be required, along with revisions to business processes and individual training. Despite the significant change involved, the potential benefit still provided a positive return on investment (ROI) with a projected breakeven in three years.

To help George and his colleagues reach these conclusions, they had to develop a deeper understanding of the firm's strategy, financial model, and competitive landscape. Since the majority of the firm's income is through B2B (business-to-business) sales via negotiated contracts, they were able to exclude analysis more typical for B2C (business-to-consumer) business models (e.g., consumer web traffic, abandoned shopping carts, click-through rates, etc.).

They realized a significant "blind spot" existed due to the lack of visibility to their market share. Once they identified a market research firm that could provide competitive sales information, they looked for innovative ways to integrate the market data with their sales transactions. They theorized that they could map their products to classes of their competitors' products. This would enable them to estimate their market share. By incorporating national demographic data, they hypothesized that they could identify underperforming geographies. These data sources were never integrated or mined for deep insights. Due to the volume and breadth of data available, they realized they'd need to integrate deep analytics and unique visualizations to understand the potential outcomes.

This entire visioning process required them to relax their traditional operating constraints and assumptions. They had to search for new ways of using existing data, new data sources, and innovative analytic methods, and embracing visual tools to help "tell the story," and accepting risks due to the breadth of the changes they were recommending. The team simplified their approach by disqualifying methods that were popular in other firms (e.g., parsing web logs).

By involving a data scientist, they also realized they could establish their long-term vision, but not firmly bound exactly how it will be realized; this is a key difference from many initiatives. The reality of constant data revelations and algorithms helped them realize they needed to "let the data guide them." Due to the new data sources, statistical methods, tools, processes, and on-going discovery, they realized an Agile approach was appropriate to maintain flexibility. Overall, this was a vastly different approach than anything they've ever recommended.

> This entire visioning process required them to relax their traditional operating constraints and assumptions.

George is also actively involved in his own personal development journey. He has been working with a coach for a number of years to continually refine his leadership skills. This coaching has supported him in successfully implementing several large scale change efforts. He is now testing as a Strategist Developmental Perspective. This is a leader who deals well with a high level of complexity and is able to work effectively with a broad range of constituent groups. Strategist Developmental Perspective is similar to the type of leadership referenced by Jim Collins in his bestselling business book *Good to Great*. This level is also referred to as "level 5 leadership." By measuring Developmental Perspective, we gain important information about a key success factor in a leader's ability to lead a complicated global change program.

The first step in leading this analytics transformation effort is to understand the foundation for the change effort (sample change foundation assessment). The following tool walks us through the analysis George uses to validate his initial hypothesis that implementing an analytics culture is in the best interest of the business and will significantly impact the strategic goal of improving operational efficiency and operating margin.

If the program is approved based on the change foundation assessment, the organization will then complete the Program Charter. Since George was successful in advocating for his program, we included the completed Program Charter after the change foundation assessment.

We are using the term program and transformation interchangeably because implementing analytics is part of the overall organizational transformation that will address not only the technology, but also the business processes and organizational mindset and culture.

Sample Change Foundation Assessment

Objective: The foundation assessment is designed to help you understand and clearly articulate why this program is being undertaken and serves as the basis for next steps in data collection. Another benefit this analysis provides is that it starts to build the foundation for the charter and the information that will be communicated in the awareness packages to new team members and change network (people who support the program on a part time or ad-hoc basis).

Data sources: Review of organizational documents, such as vision and strategic plan, and interviews with key stakeholders. To ensure a successful analytics transformation, it is critical that decision makers trust the data that is used to deliver the metrics. In addition to reviewing content, quality measurements are also taken to ensure that the best quality data is feeding the analytics engine. After initial analysis, a business case was created to support the primary foundation for the transformation. A business case captures the business need for conducting the program. It generally explains the program objectives, program investment, expected outcomes, and business value at a minimum. For large, complex, and expensive programs, companies often invest in a thorough business case analysis before taking on the investment and risk of the program. For smaller programs, the business case can be accomplished through a more rudimentary analysis and simple documentation.

Organizational vision: We are a thriving organization because our work improves the quality of life for consumers.

Strategic goals: Improve organizational profitability and product innovation

Program objectives:

- Integrate high quality corporate data sources with external market data to quantify product positioning

- Implement data mining and predictive analytics to identify and quantify price optimization opportunities

- Provide an executive dashboard to help visualize opportunities and progress

Key stakeholders:

- Executive leadership investing in the program and endorsing final decisions on data sources for the analytics products

- Pricing Analysis team to adopt new measures and processes

- Information Technology team implementing new technologies, data sources, and visualization methods

- Business units using the technology and changing work processes and adopting the information provided by the analytics
- Corporate offices using the technology and changing work processes and adopting the information provided by the analytics
- Customers who will receive more detailed analysis during price negotiations
- Investor community who will receive higher financial returns after the business case is realized

Diagnostic activities have been used to confirm the situation:

- In-depth strategic planning and analysis project identified key opportunities
- Interviews with key stakeholders to validate the need
- Developed thorough business case (during the data collection and analysis phase)
- Conducted comprehensive quality assessment for each candidate data source
- Assessment of technical and analytic skills for existing team members

Expected changes:

- Information systems
- Wide range of computer programs and manual processes
- New data sources that have not been previously integrated
- New statistical analysis methods
- Critical business processes
- Ability to adapt to change
- Where computers are located and how maintained
- Decision making processes and the quality of data available to make decisions
- Who makes decisions within organization, the level of decisions they make, and how they measure the outcome of their decisions

Consequences if changes are not implemented:

- Continued erosion of market share
- Missed price improvement opportunities
- Missed opportunity to improve competitive position within the industry
- Missed ROI targets
- Stock price impact
- Bonus/stock award impact
- Potential negative career impact for selected individuals

Approval - Who authorized the program?

- CEO
- CIO
- Business unit president
- Pricing and contract analysis director

Program Motivation:

- Improve profitability
- Identify underserved market segments
- Quantify share of market relative to competing products
- Streamline pricing process
- Improve user experience (ease of accessing and understanding data, improved metrics on utilization, interactive visualizations to understand trends)

Implementation activities:

- Educate leaders and change mindset about how to run the business
- Design processes that support overall business objectives
- Acquire new data sources
- Integrate and profile internal data to ensure usability for analytics
- Establish predictive analytic models and integrate with dashboards
- Test process effectiveness
- Prepare people for change (communicate, create excitement and buy-in, train)
- Prepare human support infrastructure (job descriptions, appraisals, compensation and rewards, sourcing, training)
- Change long-term compensation systems to reinforce system, culture, and behavioral changes required for the system to succeed

Processes in scope:

- Market penetration analysis
- Price optimization
- Contract negotiation
- Executive-level market review

Resources

- Staffing—program plan will be developed to specify number of internal staff members from each department
- Consulting support—proposals will be solicited for exact cost—ballpark estimate is a range from $x to $x to happen over the next 12 - 24 months to be clarified during detailed program planning phase

- Technology investment—to be clarified during proposal and detailed planning phase—range of investment is from $x - $x
- Leadership time to steer the program and serve as sponsors

Risk management:

- System implementation will occur in phases
- Process improvement and standardization changes will occur in conjunction with system deployment to manage performance risk and facilitate the adoption of new processes implementation
- IT changes will happen quickly after proof of concept to address security/disaster recovery related concerns (accelerate benefits of migrating off old systems and processes that incur ongoing maintenance)

Sponsors:

- CIO
- Business Unit President
- Business Unit CFO

Outcomes Upon Program Completion:

Using the business case, summarize the expected business outcomes and measures for the program.

Table 2.3

State of the organization upon successful Implementation – Populate using Strategic Plan		
Business Area	**Outcomes**	**Measures**
Business Operations	- Process changes to use quantitative analysis efficiently during the contract negotiation process - Quarterly review of contract profitability and competitive environment	- Market share - Sales volume - Profit margin - Contract review process turn time
Technical	- Integrated data warehouse updated nightly with transactional data and monthly with financial data - External market data updated monthly - Predictive analytics for sales opportunities updated weekly - Executive dashboard to summarize sales, margins, and opportunities by product and geography	- Data warehouse available at 8 a.m. Monday through Friday - Executive dashboard has all data present and responds in less than 5 seconds
Human Aspects	- Users trained on the use of interactive analytics - Market competitive analysis, sales volume and profitability are the basis of contract analysis and pricing negotiations	- Shared understanding of profitability metrics - Consistent use of new tools during review sessions

State of the organization upon successful Implementation – Populate using Strategic Plan		
Business Area	**Outcomes**	**Measures**
Leader	■ Build skills necessary to successfully implement transformation ■ Build Innovative Leadership capacity ■ Build and champion understanding of analytic processes	■ Feedback from others ■ Change successful ■ Positioned for future change success
Culture	■ Culture adopts the use of data-driven analytics to support analysis and recommendations ■ Identify culture changes needed to successfully implement and sustain the organizational benefits associated with change	■ Culture survey results ■ New culture supportive of this and successive changes ■ All recommendations are raised with supporting analysis

Sample Charter

We, as a leadership team, reviewed the change foundation assessment against the other programs presented during the planning session and approved this as one of the efforts we will be initiating this year. Based on that foundation, we created the following charter to specify to the organization, and to those involved, what would be expected from this program. Our goal was to present a high-level description and success measures giving enough information for the team to know what to do, while at the same time providing enough latitude for them to make appropriate decisions about how to accomplish the goals. The charter below reflects the Analytics Transformation program that will include many concurrent projects. We decided to break the implementation into multiple projects to minimize risk and impact to the organization.

As you are creating the charter, it will be important to consider how the program will be structured and fit within or operate outside of the traditional hierarchy.

1. Business Problem Statement

The organization is not meeting its overall growth and profitability goals. To protect the privacy of the organizations who contributed to this charter, we are not revealing details of the problem. At a high level, the problems included:

- Sales contracts not providing planned market penetration
- Extremely long, laborious preparation cycles to present accurate sales summaries
- Lack of knowledge about the competing products and market share
- Pricing negotiations driven by relationships and assumptions
- Multiple software systems that required extensive labor to reconcile data
- Inefficient processes

- Declining stock price for two years—market sending signals that our competitors are becoming more efficient than we are
- Lack of trust in metrics used in decision making process

2. Program Vision and Objectives

Ensure that key organizational changes occur in coordination with the integration of internal and external data sources. Many of these changes will need to occur using new technology and skills that will necessitate expert consultants.

There are five initial areas of focus for the program. They are listed below along with a brief description of how each area supports the overall objective of the organizational change program.

Create an Integrated, Enterprise Data Warehouse – This activity will leverage existing high-quality enterprise data assets to provide insights on our existing sales volumes by contract, product line, region, and customer. The use of this information is vital and the existing manual processes are lengthy and error prone.

Incorporate Predictive Analytics – By analyzing past utilization trends relative to contract prices, competitive trends, current sales volumes and price points across regions, predictive analytics should identify missed opportunities and geographies that are underserved. Based on the analysis, multiple price scenarios should identify customer price sensitivity based on the competing products available geographically.

Establish an Executive Dashboard – An executive dashboard will provide interactive, graphical summaries to increase awareness of sales and profit trends. By automating the population of the data from the integrated data warehouse, manual labor errors will be avoided.

Improve Analysis Used for Contract Renewal – The current contract renewal analysis process is laborious and error prone. Many of the pricing assumptions are estimates and aren't supported by price sensitivity analysis or competing products. The future state will utilize the data warehouse and predictive analytics for automated analysis.

Focus on Organization Change Management – This activity will focus on the development of streamlined processes and user training to use the new tools effectively. The organization will become comfortable using data and analytic tools to support their recommendations.

3. Success Criteria

The following are the objectives of the Organizational Transformation program:
- Sales volume increase by 5% within 6 months of contract renewal

- Contract profit margins increase by 3% within 6 months of contract renewal
- Executive dashboard provides a graphical summary of product and geographic sales, gross margin, volume relative to competing products, and underserved geographies
- Contract renewal preparation process is data and metric driven without the addition of any permanent staff
- Recommendations to improve sales volume or margins are regularly supported with quantitative analysis and scenarios within 12 months of the start of the initiative
- Expert consultants have completed the technical issues within 24 months and staff size returns to original levels
- Training on the use of quantitative methods is completed in 18 months

4. Scope

In-scope

- Acquisition of external market data
- Integration of high-quality operational systems with external data
- Development of predictive analytics
- Implementation of, and training to, support the executive and operational dashboards
- Reorganization of resources to support new processes
- Internal communication websites to support initiative and staff
- Coaching to support cultural transformation

Out-of-scope

- Implementation of additional operational systems
- Integration of subsidiaries into existing enterprise resource planning (ERP) systems
- Inclusion of new product releases
- Complete revisions to organization, geographic, or product hierarchies

5. Timeline and Deliverables

The following milestone deliverable and dates are relative to the start date of the initiative. Some deliverables are delayed due to the need to establish a foundation. Future releases can be embraced at a faster pace after we have established a baseline infrastructure.

Table 2.4

Objective	Target Date
Acquisition of external market data	Qtr 1, Year 1
Integration of high-quality internal and external data	Qtr 3, Year 1
Initial predictive model, staff training on tool use	Qtr 3, Year 1
Operational and executive dashboards	Qtr 4, Year 1
Refined predictive models, first automated contact review session	Qtr 1, Year 2
Revised dashboards	Qtr 2, Year 2
Training complete for all staff	Qtr 3, Year 2
Consultants complete knowledge transfer to staff	Qtr 4, Year 2

6. Assumptions and Constraints

Assumptions

- The program has Executive Management support and regular involvement to review progress and provide insights

- Business directors will be available in a timely manner to validate the key organizational change recommendations

- Personnel will be available to support this program as defined by the detailed program plan

- Any change to the agreed-upon scope, resource plan, schedule, and/or budget will be managed by the Change Control process

- The program team will have the ability to extract required data from all operational systems

- Program team members and operational directors will jointly develop and own the implementation checklist for incremental deployments

- Contract review staff will be able to support existing process, as well as system design, and validation sessions throughout the transition

- Staff may be realigned within geographies, but the identified geographies will remain static

- Core ERP systems will not be upgraded during the technical development phases of this initiative

- Existing infrastructure will have the capacity and processing power to integrate the new data sources

Constraints

- This program will be governed by the agreed-upon program and resource plans

- The program cost and schedule may be impacted if business and organizational change decisions are not made in a timely manner and/or do not support the program plan

7. **Interconnected Programs**

- Operational reporting program will utilize the same tools and infrastructure. Technical environmental conflicts are possible but will only degrade performance

- Deployment of a new product will occur in Qtr 3, Year 1. It will not be included in the product analysis since it won't be on existing contracts

- Year-end reporting changes will impact team members from the contract and finance teams

8. **Risks**

The following tables identifies risks, the probability of occurrence, impact, and initial mitigation strategies.

Table 2.5

Risk	Probability	Impact	Mitigation
Leadership unprepared to lead transformation program causing costly program delays, increased labor and consulting costs, and loss of employee confidence and engagement	Medium	High	Regular executive status meetings with frank feedback will be necessary. Keeping the senior leaders involved in the communication plan will maintain their commitment
Organization employees undertrained and overwhelmed by the changes, not performing their jobs properly	Medium	High	Conduct training sessions early and utilize contract review "dry runs" frequently to reinforce the training and tool use
People resist change because they are not sufficiently informed and trained	Medium	Medium	Maintain proactive communications including time to listen and address their concerns. Foster department-level change champions
Insufficient technical infrastructure	Low	Medium	Proactive testing for both capacity and quality (performance and data)

9. Communication Strategy

▰ The communication strategy will lean toward over-communicating. We'll utilize executives to initiate the transformation to ensure that everyone understands from the highest levels the need for the change.

▰ Additional messages will be prepared for all remaining leadership levels that reinforce the executive theme. As we work toward lower levels in the organization, we'll shift the messaging from informing, to listening, to collecting feedback on their needs. This will be used to help clarify and hone future messages.

▰ We will use a wide variety of media channels to ensure the themes are relayed and embraced. We'll select the most appropriate media based on the communication need, but also rotate frequently to maintain freshness. These will include but not be limited to:

  ▰ Video
  ▰ Web chat
  ▰ Newsletter
  ▰ E-mail broadcast
  ▰ Town hall meetings
  ▰ Quarterly employee meetings

10. Change Management Plan

While we want to remain flexible and adaptable, we have an organization history of analysis paralysis. To protect against that, we'll use the following change request levels to delegate as much decision making as possible. By keeping approvals near the top of the organization, the goal is to maintain the focus on rapid results.

▰ Requested changes that do not impact the delivery schedule or budget can be approved by the program team.

▰ Requested changes that impact only the delivery schedule must be approved by the Contract Analysis Director and Business Unit President.

▰ Requested changes that impact the only the budget must be approved by the CFO and Business Unit President.

▰ Requested changes that impact the budget and delivery schedule must be approved by the executive sponsors.

▰ A summary of all approved or requested changes will be reviewed at the regular status meetings.

11. Team

List team members using the following categories as a guide.

Table 2.6

Team	
Executive Sponsors	
Business Operations Sponsors	
Steering Committee Members	
Program Manager	
Business Operations Lead	
IT Lead	
Change Management Lead	
Training Lead	

12. Charter Approval Signature

By signing, sponsors acknowledge that they understood and supported the content of this document as it existed when they signed.

Table 2.7

Name	Program Roll	Signature	Date
	Executive Sponsor		
	Business Unit President		
	Director, Contract Analysis		
	CIO		
	CFO		
	Program Director		

Innovative Leadership Reflection Questions

To help you create a compelling vision and sense of urgency, it is time to further clarify your own beliefs using reflection questions. These questions are organized by quadrant to reflect the four domains introduced in Chapter One and are arranged to help you explore each of these domains. As a reminder, this is an opportunity to practice Innovative Leadership by considering how your change plan will affect your intentions, actions, culture, and systems. The questions under "What do I think/ believe?" reflect your intentions. The questions "What do I do?" reflect your actions. The questions "What do we believe?" reflect culture. The questions "How do we do this?" reflect systems. Thus, we designed this exercise to help you start practicing Innovative Leadership as you create your vision and define your direction.

The table contains several questions for each domain to be applicable to a broad range of programs. We recommend you choose two to four questions from each domain that best apply to your specific situation.

Table 2.8

QUESTIONS TO GUIDE THE LEADER AND ORGANIZATION

What do I think / believe?

- How do I see myself in the future?
- How does my view of myself impact my ability to participate in this change?
- How do I see our organization within the larger environment (ranging from the company to the global environment)?
- What are the connections between possible business futures and my personal mission, passion, and economic goals (Hedgehog Principle in *Good to Great*)?
- Why do I believe this change is urgent and necessary?
- What do I need to change about myself to lead the change successfully?
- What will I need to change about my leadership style to lead an adaptive change and corresponding business transformation?
- What is motivating me to make this change?

What do I do?

- How do I gather input from key stakeholders to incorporate into the "vision" and "sense of urgency" statements?
- How do I consider best practices when setting the vision and communicating a sense of urgency?
- How do I synthesize the competing goals and commitments to create a vision that works for the organization and is supported by multiple stakeholders?
- How do I translate the vision into long- and short-term timelines?
- How do I incorporate specific tangible goals into the timelines?
- Do I allocate the funds required to meet the program requirements and timelines?
- How will I model an appropriate response to the sense of urgency by my actions?
- What actions do I take to respond to the urgent concerns of my stakeholders?
- How will I encourage the segment(s) most likely to change without ignoring others?
- How will I explain the impact of change in a manner consistent with our culture and values?
- What stories can I use from our corporate folklore to illustrate prior examples of urgency and positive outcome?
- How can I convey messages that use emotion (personal stories) and external sources to demonstrate urgency?
- What systems must change immediately to develop a high impact organization?
- How do I set the tone that it is safe to try new things and make reasonable mistakes as we transform?

What do we believe?

- What are the organizational guiding principles?
- How does the organization see itself in the context of the larger community?
- What do we believe we stand for? What do we believe about how we should behave to accomplish what we stand for?
- How does our organizational vision fit within the larger context, i.e., community, industry?
- If you are making a change in a department of a large organization, how does the vision support the overall organization's vision?
- How do we create a belief that the vision will help the organization succeed within the larger community and also help the community succeed?
- What do my stakeholders see as urgent? Important? How does this perception vary across stakeholder groups?
- Do the employees see the need to change the culture to be more successful?
- What about the culture must change to support more effective business operations?

How do we do this?

- What is our process for determining the shared vision and values for the organization?
- What is the process for clarifying and documenting our guiding principles?
- How does the organization develop its vision taking the greater economic conditions into account (by combining an analysis of trends, our strengths, and market demand)?
- How do we understand and incorporate stakeholder priorities into the vision?
- How do we cascade the shared vision of possible futures (realistic and wild card options) to all levels of the organization?
- How do we translate the vision into a measurable work plan with goals? Who owns the specific goals?
- What measures help the organization determine progress toward goals? How do we track and report progress to these goals?
- What types of assessments are or can be performed to quantitatively determine the urgency and options? Are the assessments comprehensive in nature? Do they include input from stakeholders inside and outside of the business?
- What are the barriers and enablers that will impact success (legal, financial, building, staffing mix)?
- What systems need to be changed immediately to remove short-term barriers?
- What resources are required to succeed and how will we secure them?
- What measures should we track to understand the employees' sense of urgency so we can manage their level of distress (creating an environment that promotes change without overwhelming people)?
- How do I measure and report to stakeholders on the items they said were important?

Next, George will answer two to four reflection questions from each of the four dimensions above.

What do I think/believe?

- *Why do I believe this change is urgent and necessary?*

By understanding the competitive pressures facing our industry and studying current technology trends, I've identified a competitive advantage opportunity. Many of our competitors are studying the product position and market share, but that doesn't effectively position them to understand the market potential, how to identify it, and how to (re)position their resources. I have studied the technical approach carefully and understand how it aligns with our business challenges. I've also networked with internal and external resources to help refine the vision and gain organization alignment for the program. This is a clear result of my collaborative work preference. Due to the competitive market, our lagging financial performance, identified opportunity, and cross-department support, the senior leadership team now understands why we must seize this opportunity to catch-up with our competitors on market analysis and pass them by applying predictive analytics to pursue underserved markets with laser focus.

- *What will I need to change about my leadership style to lead an adaptive change and corresponding business transformation?*

I realize that my DEV:Q™ Job Style Assessment (that will be discussed in much greater detail in Chapter Four) indicates I'm oriented as a Strategist with a preference for Collaboration. However, I'm also aware that most of our solution delivery and operational team members test on the DEV:Q™ with a score of: Tactical: Analysts, which means they are more focused on operations and deployment with a primary focus on efficiency. I'm going to need to structure my personal communication plan to ensure I'm addressing the team members on their terms. This will require less "sales" of the strategic opportunity and greater focus on the near-term programs and their progress. I'll also need to refine the strategic messages to ensure they are loaded with specifics based on accurate product and industry measures so the team doesn't lose precious time questioning the underlying purpose or program outcomes. By ensuring I'm communicating to them on their terms, I'll maintain their support as well as help them develop an understanding of the strategic direction and competitive pressures.

Another key take-away I am beginning to understand about myself is that I am more likely to see the complex patterns required to set the vision than others around me. I need to continually remind myself that the differences in skills and focus make the assignment of roles based on this sort of assessment important. Without a clear understanding, I am likely to set people up with expectations they cannot deliver.

What do I do?

- *How do I synthesize the competing goals and commitments to create a vision that works for the organization and is supported by multiple stakeholders?*

I need to remain continuously mindful of our current financial situation. We are facing intense market pressures while sales are declining. Some stakeholders realize we must change our operating methods to achieve a different outcome. Unfortunately, many of them are linked to the single operating method they've learned. I'll need to use external stories and examples of how an analytic culture and leveraging our raw data will help us define a new trajectory. I'll also need to provide continuous updates to the executive leaders to ensure they understand the progress and how it links to our strategic goals.

- *What systems must change immediately to develop a high impact organization?*

To help establish the new practice of using trusted information to drive decisions, I'll need to expedite the transition to the use of the data warehouse and executive dashboard. This will help increase awareness of the capability and deliver a tangible result of the team's progress. By reinforcing the message on the use of information and reducing risk of a protracted solution, the key stakeholders will provide more support and realize immediate savings.

We must also consider the organizational systems that have rewarded different behavior in the past. People who held the "answers" based on their data tended to have additional power. We now make this data accessible to a much broader audience and many of them do not have, nor will they develop, the level of analytical skills required in the past to be powerful. Therefore, we will need to monitor behaviors and ensure key employees are adjusting their behavior accordingly.

What do we believe?

■ *What do my stakeholders see as urgent? Important? How does this perception vary across stakeholder groups?*

The various groups of stakeholders hold a variety of positions on this program. The executive stakeholders have a clear understanding of the need and urgency. However, they realize we don't have the internal resources or acumen to complete this transition without outside help. They also understand the need to limit investments. I'll work with them to balance the short- and long-term solutions with immediate return-on-investment to build confidence. The senior leaders don't share a consistent understanding on the program alignment with our current challenges. They'll need a separate communication plan and support from their executives to build and maintain their support. The technical and operational teams are not clear on the need for change or how to complete their future roles. They'll require substantial messages from the senior leaders, support from outside experts on the methodologies, and coaching and job aids to ensure they adopt the new processes.

By reviewing the stakeholder analysis and communication plans created by our staff, I am developing a clear understanding of each key stakeholder group. I will continue to use these tools as we move forward to better understand their objectives at each stage of the program.

■ *What about the culture must change to support more effective business operations?*

Our employees love the current culture and are comfortable with the operating processes. They are not accustomed to leveraging extensive data and analytics to support recommendations and measure decision outcome. We're going to need to provide substantial coaching and guidance to ensure they embrace the new methods. Additionally, we'll need to make sure they feel safe if they struggle with the new metrics. This can be accomplished by providing documentation, training, ask-the-expert sessions, and maintaining an open atmosphere that encourages questions. To help them embrace the impact of past decisions and build accountability, we'll need to allow them room to maneuver through past poorly supported decisions by allowing them to use analytics to indicate what should have been done. This will support the new methods, help them embrace the new tools, and not make them feel second-guessed for past decisions.

How do we do this?

- **How do we translate the vision into a measurable work plan with goals? Who owns the specific goals?**

When we chartered the program, we set out high-level goals. After conducting a high-level business case, we verified the measures needed to hit our target return on investment, so the goals were pulled from the analysis we conducted.

As we move forward, we will continue to build more detailed action plans and implementation plans that ensure we meet the return on investment (ROI) we set. I do understand that it is easy to set aside the initial assumptions and make different decisions based on more and better information. I also understand that as we gather more information, I will need to continue to verify that we are moving toward delivering a positive ROI.

Through the DEV:Q™ assessment, I realize my strength is for vision creation and limitation is for detailed execution. I'll need to work with the individual department leaders to collaboratively build the multi-phase approach. We'll need to collectively understand the sequence of deliverables that will build upon each other to provide incremental progress. Each of those deliverables will require measurements that confirm functionality as well as incremental benefits. Those measures will also help the department leaders "own" the step-by-step progress and embrace the new methods. It will be critical to gain their support and ownership of individual deliverables to ensure our successful execution as well as transformation.

- **What resources are required to succeed and how will we secure them?**

Our executive leaders realize we don't have the skills currently available or the time to build them. They have approved a budget that will enable expert consultants to build the data warehouse, predictive analytic models, and executive dashboards. While many firms have completed the integrated data warehouse in our industry, the use of predictive analytics will be a differentiator. While it may cost more, we're going to use a higher priced firm to complete all aspects since they will have a more thorough understanding of our data, processes, and organization challenges. It will also help us hold them accountable for successful outcomes at every phase of the program.

Now that you have seen George's reflection questions and his use of some foundation tools, if you are working on a change, this is the time for you to consider how you might put these or similar tools to work. If you are like most leaders, you will be tempted to complete the templates and skip the reflection questions—we strongly suggest you resist that urge. Part of the process of becoming a leader with the Developmental Perspective of Individualist or Strategist is cultivating the ability to reflect on a regular basis. We regularly hear from leaders who say they do not have any time in their day to stop and consider the broader picture. These reflection questions give you that opportunity.

Throughout this chapter, we have provided templates, processes, and examples for you to use to create a compelling vision and sense of urgency. You will use the foundation assessment to clarify the high-level details of your program and as the foundation for your charter. From there, you will proceed to create a high-level program charter. We also introduced the concept that the program team may work outside of the traditional hierarchical structure using a network-based structure that connects multiple change programs. The rest of Section II focuses on the actual process involved to bring your compelling vision into existence.

We have provided blank worksheets in the appendix for you to use on your analytics program.

What do I do?

How do we do this?

CHAPTER 3
BUILD YOUR TEAM

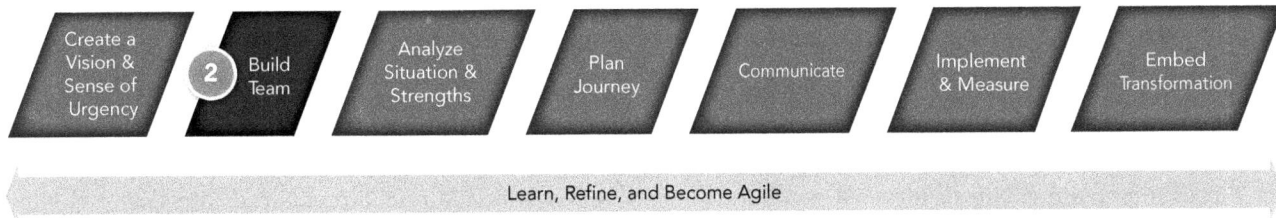

| Create a Vision & Sense of Urgency | 2 Build Team | Analyze Situation & Strengths | Plan Journey | Communicate | Implement & Measure | Embed Transformation |

Learn, Refine, and Become Agile

Select and Build your Team

Step two in the process involves determining the best people for the team, then focusing on *building* the team.

The first part is identifying who will be involved in the transformation and in which roles. *This is both a vote for who is, as well as who is not part of the transformation or on the leadership team.* So, if you are selecting a team, it will be important to understand the selection criteria. Some criteria to consider are:

- Subject matter experience and skills
- Passion, enthusiasm, and ability to influence and create buy-in
- Perceived leadership and influence in the organization
- Behavioral competencies that will allow participants to function well as part of a team and Developmental Perspective (introduced in Chapter Two)

If you have leadership issues, it is important to address them early. If there are people on the leadership team who will undermine program success, you want to make difficult decisions early. Often these people are asked to join the team because they have critical knowledge and relationships, or they are retained in roles that will not impact overall success. These are never easy actions to take, but do become an issue of managing risk as well as engagement for high-cost/high-impact programs.

The second part is building the team. By building the team, we do not mean sending an e-mail informing leaders that they now have an "extra duty;" it means dedicating time to helping team members truly understand the urgency and vision of the program and getting them excited about the impact they can make on the organization through their participation. They need to understand what is involved. After team members are selected, they will engage in team building activities to learn how to work with one another effectively on a high-demand, high-stress program.

> If you have leadership issues, it is important to address them early.

Depending on the program size and complexity, you will likely have multiple teams. These can include:

- Steering Committee – responsible for overall program oversight and success. It champions the effort, shows visible support, monitors program success, evaluates risk, and participates in major decisions

- Sponsors – responsible for providing overall support of the change (in the organization as a whole and in distributed locations at their site or location). Their actions will set the tone for the site's implementation success. If Sponsors do not "walk the talk," their employees will not believe they are committed to the program and the success of the implementation will be impacted

- Program Team – the team of people directly involved in the daily activities of accomplishing the program. For large-scale programs, key members of the program team are reassigned to the program in a full time role

- Extended Team (also known as the Change Agent Network) – people supportive of the change and credible within the organization; enlisted to help people impacted by the program understand and accept the changes they will experience

- Subject Matter Experts – ad-hoc participants involved on an as-needed basis because of their expertise

> Managing change is a challenging task. It requires highly-skilled and motivated individuals working together to achieve the business objective.

Selection Criteria

Team members are selected across a range of criteria. When change is enterprise wide, the steering committee and the program team should be selected to represent every location and line of business impacted by the change. Managing change is a challenging task. It requires highly-skilled and motivated individuals working together to achieve the business objective. Key members across all teams should be chosen with the following competencies:

- **Performance:** Is seen as an expert in their current position; can set aside personal agendas, desires, and biases that might hinder the success of the program

- **Communication:** Has excellent communication skills and is comfortable speaking with all levels and functions across the organization

- **Teamwork:** Can develop a high level of teamwork with key players in this implementation; is a team player and is comfortable leading or following as necessary

- **Credibility:** Must have a successful history in the organization with no political liabilities

- **Trust:** Must act and speak in ways to facilitate trusting relationship with sponsors and targets

- **Culture:** Has knowledge of multiple cultures within business units and locations

- **Commitment:** Will demonstrate understanding and commitment to the overall enterprise changes; must understand how program supports overall changes and acts as a champion within the organization at all levels to communicate and support program success and realization of business benefits

- **Innovative Leadership:** Developmental Perspective and Leadership Behaviors (introduced in Chapter One) must be aligned with the program expectations.

- **Commitment to Personal Development:** Willing to engage in coaching and development activities to build knowledge and expertise required to lead complex adaptive change.

After you select your team members, it will be important to communicate expectations and build the group into a team with a clear plan with specific expectations. Following is an example of a high-level sponsor plan. These plans will summarize expectations of the individuals playing each role. You will want a similar plan for each of the teams (using the previous list or other variations of teams).

In addition to creating a charter, it is important to get everyone together to kick-off or launch the project. We realize that in a global organization this may not be possible and may need to be handled by teleconference. At minimum, this session should include the following:

- **On the task side:**
  - Clear performance expectations
  - Clear understanding of measures
  - Understanding participant benefits for taking on this role (this could be company benefit in the case of senior leaders who are often compensated by bonus and is often different than the program team member who may be building skills toward promotion)
  - Understanding sense of urgency—what is in it for them

- **On the relationship side:**
  - Understand personality type and/or leadership competency of individuals and how they best contribute
  - Understand the "personality type" of the group so you understand how you fit with the group—your strengths, as well as how to handle potential challenges
  - Establish how you want to work together
  - Understand individual strengths
  - Begin to develop supportive alliances and friendships based on mutual interest, strengths, and trust

Tools

One of the first steps in this phase is having each person identify their "draft picks" using this worksheet or other format. The purpose of this process is to identify who would be a best fit against our selection criteria.

Table 3.1

Criteria	Functional Expertise Y/N	Communication Y/N	Teamwork Y/N	Credibility Y/N	Trust Y/N	Culture Y/N	Commitment Y/N	Developmental Perspective (Level)	Commitment to Develop Y/N
Selection Matrix									
Steering Committee									
Chair									
Member									
Member									
Sponsors									
Team Members									
Program Manager									
Team Leads									

Team Plans

After you identify who is on the teams, you will want to create plans for each of the teams explaining their responsibilities, measures, and how you will work to engage them in the program. The following is a table showing a sample of items that may be included. Different organizations will include different components, but this list serves as a solid starting point. According to the McKinsey research, about the top six tactics for change success referenced at the beginning of the book, one objective is establishing well-defined stretch targets. By creating individual and team objectives, learning objectives, and responsibilities, participants understand what is expected and how they will meet their goals.

> By creating individual and team objectives, learning objectives, and responsibilities, participants understand what is expected and how they will meet their goals.

Table 3.2

Team objectives
Team learning objectives
Major deliverables
Responsibilities
Engagement
Timing
Measure of success
Resource requirements

After the charters are created, it will be important to have a team building or launch. Among tools that will support this process will be a team assessment. Most teams find that they benefit greatly by using a skilled facilitator—who is not part of the team—to plan and facilitate the session. This person should have a strong ability to understand and navigate complex team dynamics. Tools for the session will include:

- Discussion of objectives and roles and responsibilities to clarify the work of the team

- Team dynamics are also an important component of the kick-off
    - Enneagram individual and composite team assessment
    - LCP or other 360° individual and team composite assessment

Stories and Examples

When organizations are too large to have all locations included, you will want to consider how you group locations such as regions or countries. When you cannot include everyone, include those who are most impacted. Today's world and virtual meeting capabilities make a HUGE difference in who can and will participate. Guidelines such as having everyone have their video on for meetings bring a new level of interaction and commitment.

In selecting your team, you will want to leverage the assessment results, and this is one of the areas in which the transformation steps will be happening concurrently. You may want to begin assessing your leaders using key assessment tools (referenced in Chapter Four) prior to finalizing team selection if you have questions, for example, about Developmental Perspective. These tools provide valuable insight about how you might expect people to work together, and they are just the first part of building a team. Using assessments provides an important start and team members need to do the work to build a solid foundation quickly so when they encounter challenges as always happens on complex projects, they have the capacity to navigate them without unnecessary time loss or loss of trust that could derail progress.

If you do not have leaders who are at the Individualist or Strategist Developmental Perspective (using the framework provided by the MAP assessment tool), which is unlikely in large complex organizations, you can leverage consultants, and/or you may have people at these later developmental perspectives who are not on the leadership team. If this is the case, you will want to position these people as trusted advisors to the sponsor team rather than voting members of the team.

Let's return to George as he selects his sponsor team. George has evaluated the range of leaders within his organization and has made sure he has people from most functional units and locations, and also has at least one person at the Strategist Developmental Perspective (which is him). This team selection process is a tough one because he needs to attend to skills, behavioral characteristics, region, Developmental Perspective, and team size. He wanted a team of twelve or fewer. He ended up with ten people he thought would be effective as the steering committee.

He then worked with that steering committee to select the program team and the sponsor team. He will look to the sponsors to select the extended team as the program progresses and to determine how to best leverage the extended team's involvement.

Following is a subset of the sponsor plan George worked with the steering committee to create.

Sponsorship Plan

Objective: The Sponsorship Plan addresses the need to have executives throughout the organization leading the change. It will serve as the activity road map. Sponsors will help each group of users understand and embrace the change program and the business goals driving the program. Sponsors will ensure that the planned changes deliver the intended benefits for the organization.

Sponsors are responsible for providing overall support of the change at their site. Their actions will set the tone for the site's implementation success. Because of the impact these activities have on project acceptance, you may find that you want to engage professional support such as marketing to help implement some of the actions in the plan.

Sponsors are responsible for providing overall support of the change at their site. Their actions will set the tone for the site's implementation success.

Major Deliverables:

- Create sponsorship plans

- Facilitate sponsor education material and action plans

- Conduct ongoing follow-up with sponsors

- Create metrics to gauge change readiness

- Resource requirements

Table 3.3

Activity	When	Message	Primary Objective
Steering Committee Action			
Steering Committee Meets with Sponsor		■ Explain expectations for: ▪ Participation (specific behaviors) ▪ Results ▪ Level of authority, accountability, and control ▪ Project Involvement ▪ Rewards/consequences	■ Create a mutual understanding of responsibility, commitment, and authority for implementing the program ■ Define consequences of success and failure
Create Steering Committee Video, Posters and Newsletter Article Outlines		■ Explain benefits of the program ■ Explain how project links to other organizational objectives ■ Reinforce key reasons to support the change ■ Support the transition process	■ Create a consistent message of executive support and explain why this is important to overall organizational performance
Site / Location Sponsor (for programs that have multiple locations)			
Sponsor Initial Meeting	Jan.	■ Interview to determine past transition history and what should be done differently on this program ■ Determine what the manager wants to get from this implementation (business benefits and what keeps him up at night) ■ Discuss specific action steps and determine type of support we can provide ■ Discuss best practices and/or lessons learned to shape their thinking (based on data)	■ Understand specific barriers and create a plan to manage these ■ Understand motivators to craft messages and solutions that address specific concerns ■ Begin to create sponsor action plan ■ Build understanding of actions necessary to create success

Sponsor Meeting with Direct Reports	Feb.	■ Administer Change Foundation Scorecard and score in the group ■ Discuss specific action steps for change success ■ Create an action plan	■ Create an understanding of infrastructure and processes necessary for change success ■ Develop action plan to address open issues
Sponsor Kick-off Site Steering Committee	Feb.	■ Conduct steering committee meeting and discuss expectations of program, reporting, expectations for level of authority and desired involvement	■ Set the expectation that this program is critical to company success, clarify expectations, measures, and involvement

Sponsor Kick-off Implementation Team	May	■ Attend and present at the implementation team kick-off meeting
		  ■ Discuss importance of the program, what he expects of them, and what they can expect of him
		  ■ Motivational
			■ Set the expectation that this program is critical to company success, clarify expectations, measures, and involvement
			■ Build momentum and commitment

Sponsor Meet with Teams Monthly for Status and Support	Monthly/ bi-weekly	■ Track progress, make decisions, approve high-level direction	■ Show support ■ Validate progress ■ Take corrective action
Sponsor Kick-off General Roll-out Session(s)	June – Oct.	■ Attend and present at the Overall Kick-Off meeting(s) ■ Discuss importance of the program, what he expects of them, and what they can expect of him ■ Motivational	■ Set the expectation that this program is critical to their success, clarify expectations, measures, and involvement ■ Build momentum and commitment
Sponsor Discusses Program in Ongoing Company Meetings	Ongoing	■ Present program status, recent accomplishments, success stories, and what to expect	■ Move entire organization from aware that this is happening to an understanding and clarity about how they will contribute
Sponsor Publicly Acknowledges Wins	TBD	■ Acknowledge contribution and accomplishments of the program team	■ Build momentum and commitment ■ Give people an incentive to participate ■ Create understanding of benefits of the program
Monthly Status Call with PMO	Monthly	■ Status update two-way ■ People management: how are they doing, and how are we managing their careers	■ Build understanding and commitment ■ Identify barriers and address issues ■ Provide career opportunities to program team members to build commitment
Measure Change Readiness	Monthly July – Oct.	■ Use Change Foundation Scorecard and Change Readiness Scorecard ■ Refine action plan ■ Measure progress on plan	■ Establish baseline ■ Determine corrective action ■ Track action items

Innovative Leadership Reflection Questions

To help you define who should be involved in the program, it is time to further clarify your direction using reflection questions. These questions are organized to reflect the four domains introduced in Section I. As a reminder, this is an opportunity to practice Innovative Leadership by considering how your change plan will affect changes in your intentions, actions, culture, and systems. These questions are arranged to help you explore each of these domains. The questions for "What do I think/believe?" reflect your intentions. The questions "What do I do?" reflect your actions. The questions "What do we believe?" reflect culture. The questions "How do we do this?" reflect systems. Thus, we designed this exercise to help you start practicing Innovative Leadership as you create your vision and define your direction.

The table contains several questions for each domain to be applicable to a broad range of programs. We recommend you choose two to four questions from each domain that best apply to your specific situation.

Table 3.4

QUESTIONS TO GUIDE THE LEADER AND ORGANIZATION

What do I think / believe?
- Do I believe the change is good for those I am inviting to participate?
- How will my behaviors and beliefs impact others success?
- Do I believe the people on the teams are being positioned for success?
- Do I believe participating in this program will be helpful for the careers of the people involved?
- Do I believe we have key leaders involved who will interfere with program success including demotivating employees on the program team?

What do I do?
- How do I determine and communicate the criteria for "right" people on the team? ("Right" includes character traits, innate capabilities, and skills and knowledge.)
- How do I place the "right" people in charge of the biggest opportunity (not the biggest problem)? How do I recruit them for this personal and business transformation?
- What comments and actions will demonstrate my belief that change is possible?
- Am I looking for opportunities to visibly support the program as events unfold?
- What am I doing to retain the participants in the company and on the program?
- How do I lead a team based on the task at hand? Am I focused sufficiently on running the business while still attending to the change (personal and organizational)?
- Do I need to make difficult staffing decisions that would involve removing (not selecting) key leaders for roles?

What do we believe?
- What are the social and cultural norms that dictate who should be leading the program?
- How do we use the program as an opportunity to test new behaviors and demonstrate their positive impact on the organization?
- Do current social and cultural norms still fit for where we are going?
- Do people leading the change have the right support to change the culture as appropriate?
- How do we engage people in our organization to promote involvement and adoption?

> **How do we do this?**
>
> - What are the key skills and behaviors necessary for the organization to transform? What are the gaps between our current staff and the staff needed to support transformation? Does the organization have people available with the right skills and behaviors?
> - What is the best combination of approaches to allow us to meet staffing needs, including hiring, reassignments, temps, and consultants?
> - Does our hiring strategy support attracting the type of people we are trying to find? Are we asking the right questions in the interview process to select people who can successfully implement change?
> - What trust building activities can we conduct to improve team dynamics?
> - What measures should we track to reinforce desired team behaviors? Personal and professional changes?
> - If the transformation is a long one, how are team members rewarded for their effort and risk? What happens if a team member does not thrive in the program environment?
> - Am I communicating what stakeholders believe is important to the team?
> - What is the process that supports selection of team members? Are they formalized? What are the criteria that will support team success?

In preparation for selecting team members, George answered the reflection questions. He anticipated that he would need to make some tough decisions and knew that this reflection process would help him think through some of those issues in advance of the meeting at which team members would be "drafted."

What do I think/believe?

- ### How will my behaviors and beliefs impact others success?

   As a strong leader with a passion for measurable outcomes, I need to remain mindful that our culture favors comfort and consistency. If I continue to "sell" the vision and drive for results without bringing along the technical and operational delivery teams, I risk losing support for the transformation. It's important to remember that driving too hard for the change may drive the team away. I'll need to allow time to work with the team to understand their progress on the transition and trust in the use of information and analytics. Similarly, if I don't continuously refresh the executive team on how the transition is providing tangible results, they'll lose faith and potentially terminate the program. I'll need to ensure that I provide complete transparency as well as "sell" the next phases with a strong linkage to overcoming our immediate challenges.

- ### Do I believe we have key leaders involved who will interfere with program success including demotivating employees on the program team?

   As we selected the sponsors, we were careful to select individuals that are able to work as change champions. This will make it easier to develop and adopt the new methods. While it is risky, we've also included a member that is change averse. He strongly prefers our current methods and is vocal in his opposition, but is willing to have rational discussions. He is key to the program success due to his vocal nature and influence on the operations team. If we remove him abruptly, we will violate the cultural norm and send an adverse message to team members that question the need for the change. By keeping him on the sponsor team and having him help craft and deliver messages, we'll be able to embrace his feedback and influence the message he delivers. This will ultimately help the operations team accept the changes. It will require substantial effort to ensure his formal and informal communications remain consistent.

I also realized that unlike other initiatives I've led, this analytics transformation requires a more carefully balanced team. In many initiatives, we focus on visionary leaders, process design experts, and IT. In this transformation, we're more deeply involved in statistical analysis, quantitative methods, unique visualizations, staff training, and process innovation. This has required much broader involvement from more leaders. To ensure their on-going commitment, it has required significantly more communications throughout all levels in the organization.

What do I do?

■ *What comments and actions will demonstrate my belief that change is possible?*

Many of the team members are concerned about their part in the future organization. By acknowledging that it is an important transformation and talking about my support of the change will provide consistently visible action. The other visible action I am taking is to attend all key meetings and actively participating—continually reinforcing how important this program is to our overall strategic direction and profitability.

I am also seeking outside examples and experts to ensure our success. These experts include a heavy reliance on consultants; some will bring technical expertise and others change management experience. My actions will make it easier for others on the team to embrace outside perspectives to enable their personal journey. It will require a fine balance of a reaffirming message as well as a level of humility that even I need to embrace the unknown and push forward into unchartered territory.

■ *Am I looking for opportunities to visibly support the program as events unfold?*

While providing transparent progress reports, I'll need to be vigilant about sharing successes and allowing team members to claim that success. By allowing them to take the credit, they'll have more ownership for ensuring the changes "stick," and the business benefit is acknowledged.

As the program proceeds, I am continually looking for events within the company and in our industry that reinforce the importance of leveraging analytics. Last week, I came across an article in one of our key online industry journals talking about how an analytics program implemented by another firm created a significant improvement in ability to meet customer needs proactively. This specific case study impacted inventory ordering and reduced cost significantly. By finding tangible examples and even better tying them to things we care about like inventory management and customer satisfaction, I will help people move from understanding of the program to acceptance and maybe even excitement.

What do we believe?

- ### *How do we use the program as an opportunity to test new behaviors and demonstrate their positive impact on the organization?*

It is important to first create a safe environment where people can try new behaviors and feel supported. This is particularly important when people are asked to take on new roles where they have limited experience. In some instances, we have implemented partial changes in advance of system change to allow the impacted staff to space out the impact over time and build competence so they feel safe and the project risk is diminished.

By focusing on incremental deliverables and immediate use of those features, we can give the teams time to adopt the new methods and behaviors. It will also allow us to measure both the outcome and their progress on embracing the tools and processes. Since the organization embraces consistency, this will hopefully lead to an early adoption of tools and data which will be the new "norm." A key element for the senior leadership team will be incorporating measures of tool use as part of the tool delivery.

- ### *Do people leading the change have the right support to change the culture as appropriate?*

The steering committee and sponsors have been fully empowered to change the processes and culture on their teams. It helps that we've transferred the ownership of phases and business outcomes to them. While we collectively report progress to the executive team, they are both empowered and accountable for ensuring adoption of the new methods. Much of that outcome will be intuitively measured with their operational progress reports using the new tools and supporting their recommendations.

How do we do this?

- ### *What measures should we track to reinforce desired team behaviors? Personal and professional changes?*

During implementation, we will be conducting a change readiness assessment at various stages (this is discussed in further detail in Chapter Four). We can quantify the shift in acceptance based on various activities. We will also track task participation such as training attendance and pilot system usage.

As program phases are completed and new tools are deployed (with corresponding business processes), we will measure adoption by ensuring the tools are used during contract review meetings. The executives are expecting results to be more quantitative and will be expecting the tools to be used. We can measure individual progress by having them support their analysis and recommendations with data via the new systems. The new methods will take time to adopt, but with public use through regular meetings, progress will be easily demonstrated and measured.

■ *If the transformation is a long one, how are team members rewarded for their effort and risk? What happens if a team member does not thrive in the program environment?*

Team member progress will be measured through tool use and process adoption. With successful presentations and supported recommendations, we'll celebrate these with published success stories. Personal recognition will provide strong peer support for embracing change. For people motivated by being early adopters and technical wizards, they will be the first to use the new tools so these selection criteria will play to their innate preferences. Participating in the program will provide an innate reward.

We expect that not all team members will embrace this transition. We will provide substantial training and coaching, but not all team members will have the aptitude. Other teams in the organization will not require analytic skills, and we'll embrace finding appropriate roles for as many team members as possible.

After the selection process, George indicated that he was glad he took the time to reflect on his choices as it did impact some of his decisions. He is also becoming more aware of how important this type of personal development is to allow him to successfully implement the large volume of change required to realize full value from this implementation. He is aware of the risks he faces as a key leader in making a wrong decision and the impact that it can have. He is addressing some of that risk by being part of a steering team that has invested in building a solid working relationship as they had not all worked together in the past. There is, in fact, some expectation that people will make mistakes. The team uses solid project management practices to manage key risks. Additionally, recruiting the right team early (right skills and behaviors) reduces the likelihood of mistakes that derail the project.

If you are working on a change initiative and at the phase where you are selecting your team, it is time for you to answer the reflection questions. Again, we encourage you to answer the reflection questions along with using the selection criteria to identify the best candidates for the role.

Throughout this chapter, we have discussed criteria for team members at various levels within the program as well as provided reflection questions. This should serve as the foundation for you to make decisions on who to include on the team in multiple capacities.

We have provided blank worksheets in the appendix for you to use on your analytics program.

What do I think/believe?

What do I do?

What do we believe?

CHAPTER 4
ANALYZE YOUR SITUATION AND STRENGTHS

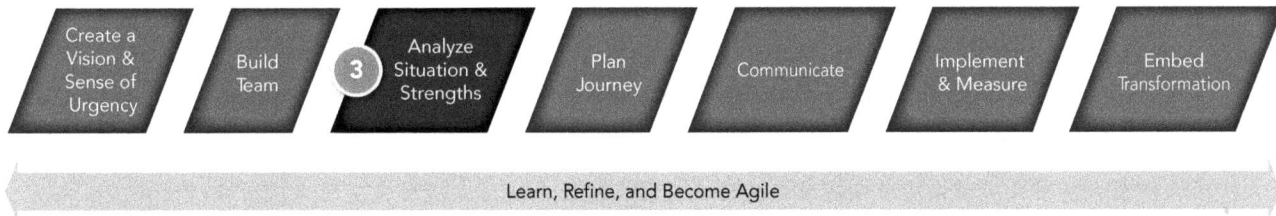

| Create a Vision & Sense of Urgency | Build Team | 3 Analyze Situation & Strengths | Plan Journey | Communicate | Implement & Measure | Embed Transformation |

Learn, Refine, and Become Agile

Now that you have begun developing and clarifying your transformation initiative based on the vision, charter, and selection of team members, it is time to collect data that will serve as the foundation for planning activities. For some of you, you began collecting data in prior steps, and you will now identify additional data. The combination of the vision and your understanding and analysis of the current state will give you a solid foundation to determine the gaps between where you are now and where you want to be. This chapter will help you understand the range of assessments you will want to consider in evaluating your current state and change readiness. In a large-change program, this phase can take several months.

It is important to combine your vision with a firm understanding of the four key dimensions of your situation to create a complete picture of your as-is state. These four dimensions are:

- Leader intentions
- Behaviors
- Organizational culture
- Systems

> It is important to get a snapshot of transformation readiness in each of the four areas.

These elements will be the key components of the transformation effort. This data will help you clarify what needs to change within the organization and what you need to change about yourself to successfully lead the change. The assessments will give you clear information about your current state. This information in conjunction with your vision will help you confirm and refine the program scope.

To ensure assessments are comprehensive, they must capture data from each of those four domains. It is important to get a snapshot of transformation readiness in each of the four areas. Many organizations are already using assessment tools that cover several of these areas.

Table 4.1

ASSESSMENT OVERVIEW

Leader Mindset – Am I able to successfully lead a complex change? Does my Type and Developmental Perspective match with the program responsibilities?

- Evaluate leader's ability to lead the change – leadership competencies associated with transformation and Developmental Perspective

- Evaluate individual attitudes toward the change and willingness – individual change readiness

- Evaluate individual ability to change – individual capacity to change

Recommended Tools: Enneagram (Leader Type), MAP Assessment or DEV:Q™ (Developmental Perspective), change readiness assessment

Leader Behavior – How do my actions impact the program success? Do my Leadership Behaviors align with the program requirements?

- Observe how leaders model critical behaviors associated with a successful transformation such as open exploration of issues and alternatives for existing constraints

- Observe how leaders create a shared vision across multiple groups within the organization

Observe individual outcomes and their contribution to overall program goals

Recommended Tools: Metcalf & Associates Resilience assessment and Leadership Circle Profile 360 Assessment (Leadership Behaviors) or custom leadership 360° addressing mindset competencies (referenced in Chapter One)

Organizational Culture – How does our culture support and inhibit the program success?

- Evaluate the organization's culture against cultures that support successful transformation and determine the gap using a culture assessment

- Identify opportunities of focus

Recommended tool Metcalf & Associates Culture Gap Analysis

What systems, procedures, and processes do we need to put in place to ensure success?

- Evaluate stakeholder impact to determine how the program will affect them and when to plan communication, training, and job change activities by stakeholder group

- Evaluate business performance using clearly established metrics and process owners

- Evaluate the organizational structure and determine what is necessary to support the desired program outcomes that fit within the future organizational norms

- Conduct Team Effectiveness Assessment to determine process and organizational system changes that would support program success

- Evaluate organization's readiness to adapt to change

- Evaluate the current communication tools and frequency as foundation for program communication plan

- Assess job changes on key roles including task change and workload changes

- Determine risk of the change initiative on the business – identify items such as Day 1 risks as well as program risks

- Technology tools assessment – identify what technological tools you will need to acquire to facilitate the change initiative

- Provide consequences for performance

Recommended tools:

- *Stakeholder Impact Assessment*
- *User Impact Analysis*
- *Existing Business Scorecard*
- *Team Effectiveness Assessment*
- *Change Readiness Assessment*
- *Risk Assessment*
- *Communication Survey*
- *Quality Assessment*
- *Change Readiness Assessment*
- *Technology Tools Assessment*
- *Change History*
- *Change Initiative Inventory*
- *Change Foundation Scorecard*
- *Change Alignment Scorecard*

Assessment Tools

Now that we have presented assessments from the four different dimensions, you will have the opportunity to select those that best meet your needs and determine how best to use the results. It is important to remember the balancing act between investing time and money in assessments so you can ensure you are making sound decisions with the expectation of your constituents that you deliver results quickly. This is a balancing act that all programs face. We tend to look for opportunities to deliver quick results while time phasing the assessments and building comprehensive plans that will truly support program success. One of the important elements of assessments is that it is an early opportunity to engage multiple stakeholders in order to understand their perspective and begin building support for the program. People tend to commit to programs when their opinion is sought in ways that respect their time and expertise.

We will start with leader assessments then move to culture and organizational assessments. As a reminder: if leaders are trying to implement changes that are adaptive (complex changes that require the leaders to change themselves in the process of changing the organization), they will sub-optimize the program outcome if they are not personally growing and adapting. Because program changes are often asking leaders to step into new ways of thinking and new roles, it is important to assess them as the foundation for leader development and coaching as part of the overall program plan.

> If leaders are trying to implement changes that are adaptive (complex changes that require the leaders to change themselves in the process of changing the organization), they will sub-optimize the program outcome if they are not personally growing and adapting.

It is important to note that how others perceive you is based, in part, on their own values and overall view of the world. Interpreting assessment data, particularly input from others, can be just as much an art as science. Rather than taking such feedback at face value, we suggest trying to understand the stance of those evaluations, as well as the culture of the organization. Generally, the data and feedback are the beginning of an analytical process for you, as the leader, to determine what changes are most aligned with your goals and those of the organization.

For example, if an individual is results-oriented in a culture that prefers collaboration, that individual may be perceived as having a negative disposition: controlling, driven, and autocratic. Alternatively, another organization with a different culture more aligned with a results-driven approach may perceive that same individual as being extremely positive: achieves results, vision-focused, and system-oriented. Part of understanding development and effectiveness is finding an organization that aligns with your leadership style, as well as a culture that can support your potential to grow.

It is helpful to take multiple assessments at the same time to paint a more complete and accurate picture of who you are as a leader. For example, the Enneagram shows your personality type, the DEV:Q™ shows your fit for a specific type of role, and MAP shows your ability to take multiple perspectives associated with levels of development, and the TLCP shows how you are perceived by others as well as how you see yourself. Taking multiple assessments allows you to better understand your innate skills and abilities as well as your opportunities. This comprehensive information allows you to determine how you can best support the transformation effort. Keep in mind that interpreting the data from these and other assessments requires specialized expertise, and we strongly recommend working with a certified coach. Similar to getting medical tests, the potential value of the information is only realized with proper translation. To that end, having a coach interpret the series of assessments as the foundation for your development plan and organizational role can significantly increase your results, because you will know exactly where to focus your efforts.

> Taking multiple assessments allows you to better understand your innate skills and abilities as well as your opportunities.

There are several good assessments available. We have used the suggested tools extensively with our clients and recommend them with a high degree of confidence. Moreover, we find that each tool provides vital information in helping to convey a comprehensive picture of strengths, weaknesses, and opportunities. These assessments are aligned with the five key components of Innovative Leadership elements discussed in Section I of the book. There are many highly reliable and effective tools beyond what we suggest, and we recommend that you explore additional tools that feel right to you.

We will now review a subset of the tools provided in Table 4.1 – Assessment Overview. These tools are broken into the same groups as in the prior table so you can track progress.

Leader Mindset – Type and developmental perspectives significantly influence how you see your role and function in the workplace, how you interact with other people, and how you solve problems. The term "Developmental Perspective" can be described as "meaning making," or how you make meaning or sense of experiences. This is important because the algorithm you use to make sense of the world influences your thoughts and actions. Incorporating these perspectives as part of your inner exploration is critical to shaping Innovative Leadership.

> Type and developmental perspectives significantly influence how you see your role and function in the workplace, how you interact with other people, and how you solve problems.

The primary reason for leadership development is that it significantly impacts an organization's ability to successfully implement a business transformation, and the associated process and cultural transformation. According to Rooke and Torbert in separate articles:

> *"In ten longitudinal organizational development efforts, the five CEOs measuring at the late Strategist/Leader stage (Level 5 Leaders) of development supported 15 progressive organizational transformations. By contrast, the five CEOs measuring at pre-Strategist stages (levels below Level 5) of development supported a total of 0 progressive organizational transformations (no change in two organizations; a three stage regression in one organization; and three stages of progressive development in two organizations). The progressively transforming organizations became industry leaders on a number of business indexes. The three organizations that did not progress developmentally lost personnel, industry standing, and money as well."*

—Rooke, David and William R. Torbert,
"Organizational Transformation as a Function of CEOs' Developmental Stage."
Organization Development Journal 16, 1998

> *"Only the final 15% of managers in the sample showed the consistent capability to innovate and successfully transform their organizations."*

—Rooke, David and William R. Torbert,
"Seven Transformations of Leadership, Leaders are made, not born, and how they develop is critical for organizational change," *Harvard Business Review,* April 2005.

- **Leader Type Assessment using the Enneagram.** We recommend using the Enneagram first and foremost to discover your own personality type and (where possible) to ascertain the types of those with whom we are interacting. The Enneagram is used for personal growth, relationships, therapy, or in the business world as an indicator of an individual's primary personality type. As you read in Section I, having an accurate understanding of type can be helpful. The Riso-Hudson Enneagram Type Indicator (version 2.5) provides a reliable, independently scientifically validated tool for that purpose. Please remember that discovering your type is only the first step in the process of self-discovery and working with this system.

Finding your type is not the final goal, but merely the starting place for a fascinating and rewarding journey of self-reflection.

The Enneagram helps you see your own personality dynamics more clearly. Once you are aware of the importance of personality types, you see that your own style will not be equally effective with everyone. Thus, one of the most useful lessons of the Enneagram is how to move from a style of interacting in which others are expected to mold themselves to your way of thinking and values, to a more flexible style in which you act from an awareness of the strengths and potential contributions of others. By doing so, you help others become more effective themselves—and, as a result, harmony, productivity, and satisfaction are likely to increase (source: www.enneagraminstitute.com/practical. asp). The Enneagram report is a text-based report that provides the leader's score for each type since leaders' results will encompass some of each type with one or more dominant types.

- Developmental Perspective – To evaluate developmental perspectives we use the **Maturity Assessment Profile (MAP)** based on the **Leadership Maturity Framework (LMF)**. This developmental toolset was created by Susanne Cook-Greuter as part of her doctoral dissertation at Harvard, and we use them as the foundation for our developmental discussion. This is widely considered one of the most rigorously validated, reliable, and advanced assessment tools used to evaluate adult leadership development. Participants taking the assessment complete 36 sentence stems (e.g., When someone needs help…?). The freeform response format allows test takers to give a broad range of information that provides the scorer ample data with which to evaluate varying developmental features along three main lines: cognitive complexity, emotional affect, and behavioral/action logic. Action logic is how people tend to reason and respond to life. It is critical for the test subject to be completely open and honest when taking this assessment in order for the scorer to have sufficient data to provide an accurate score.

> Once you are aware of the importance of personality types, you see that your own style will not be equally effective with everyone.

We included sample feedback below to illustrate the leader's results across a bell shaped curve.

Figure 4.1: Sample Feedback from the MAP

Stage	Distribution of 36 responses by sentence #
Impulsive	-
Opportunist	-
Diplomat	-
Expert	17, 23, 29, 32, 34, 35
Achiever	6, 9, 11, 18, 21, 24, 26, 27
Individual	1, 2, 3, 5, 7, 8, 12, 13, 15, 20, 22, 25, 28, 31, 33
Strategist	10, 14, 19, 30, 36
Magician	5
Ironist	-

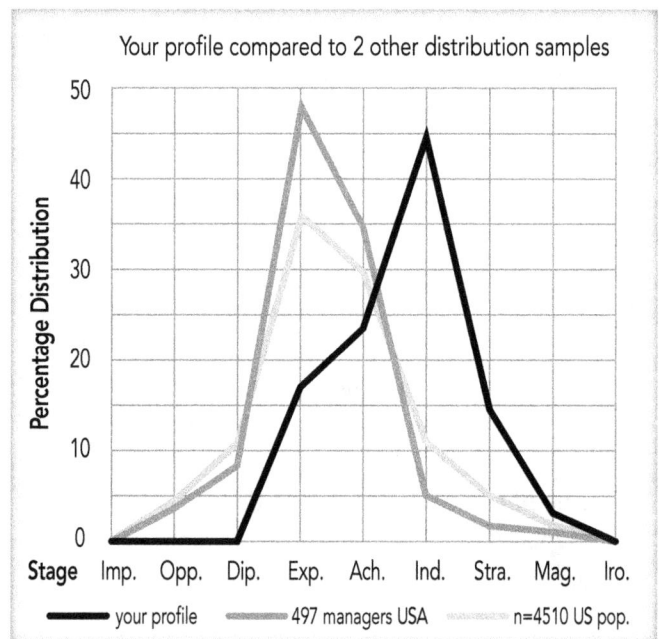

Your profile compared to 2 other distribution samples

Percentage Distribution

Stage: Imp. Opp. Dip. Exp. Ach. Ind. Stra. Mag. Iro.

— your profile — 497 managers USA n=4510 US pop.

The second tool we recommend is the DEV:Q™ Job Style Assessment to better understand your performance orientation, or the unique patterns you use to translate information, manage tasks, and engage in teams. This assessment is a hybrid assessment that points to development but is not a thorough developmental assessment as it focuses primarily on observable behavior rather than the more robust psychological analysis. This assessment is highly valuable because it helps you understand where your performance patterns fit into different job roles. These patterns correlate to capabilities needed at key levels of work common to all organizations. Based on over 50 years of social-behavioral research, the DEV:Q™ Job Style Assessment algorithm evaluates your performance style along a spectrum (efficiency drives versus innovation drives), and classifies your capability into one of four performance levels and nine prototypes, each with a dominant inclination toward specific types of tasks, roles, and outcomes. The DEV:Q™ Job Style Assessment is cost-effective, with 24 questions and only 20 minutes to take online. This assessment provides an online immediate response and a coach is not required but still advised. It is a nice complement to the MAP.

Figure 4.2: Sample DEV:Q™ Feedback

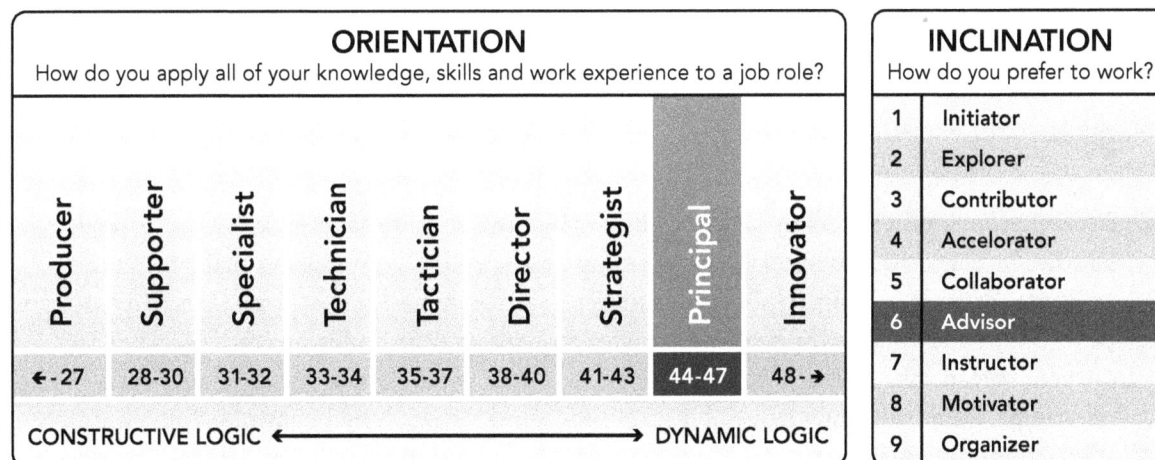

If you take the DEV:Q™ assessment as you proceed through this workbook, you will find that if you test as "visionary" on this assessment, you will likely score well on the seven leadership competencies referenced in Chapter One. It is important to note that few leaders will actually test as having all of these mindset competencies. That number is likely less than five percent of current organizational managers and leaders. This means as leaders of complex change, we have a clearer view of what is required to implement successful transformation so we can focus our leadership development efforts in areas that will have the greatest impact.

Leader Behavior – Both resilience and an assessment of behavioral competencies are helpful to identify a leader development plan to accompany the organizational development plan.

1. *Resilience* – As a leader, you need to be physically and emotionally healthy to do a good job. In addition to physical and emotional health, the resilient leader also has a clear sense of life purpose and strong supportive relationships. For most people, enhancing resilience requires a personal change. We maintain that creating and maintaining resilience is essential to your success. As you improve your resilience, you will think more clearly and have a greater positive impact in your interactions with others; investing in your resilience supports the entire organization's effectiveness.

> Effective Leadership Behaviors drive organizational success and conversely ineffective Leadership Behaviors drive organizational dysfunction or failure.

Metcalf & Associates created a tool to help you assess personal attitudes and practices that help support resilience and identify those areas where you can further build your capacity. It is based on fundamental stress management research, including the characteristics that support "stress hardiness," a concept pioneered by Kobasa, and research by Gallup and the Human Performance Institute on the Corporate Athlete. (Refer to Section I, Chapter Three on Resilience for more extensive details. This assessment is available on the Metcalf & Associates web site www.metcalf-associates.com.)

2. *Leader Behavior* – Leadership skills and hard skills are critical to success, and serve as objective performance measures of Innovative Leadership. Hard skills fall into two primary categories: industry-related knowledge, skills, and aptitudes; and functional knowledge, skills, and aptitudes. Leadership behaviors are the result of knowledge, skills, and aptitudes specifically related to the craft of leadership. We will be using the term Leadership Behaviors in this book when referring to leadership knowledge, skills, aptitudes, and the resulting behaviors. Both hard skills and Leadership Behaviors are critical to organizational transformation. The balance between the importance of hard skills and Leadership Behaviors will shift as the leader progresses in the organization with these skills and behaviors becoming increasingly important with career advancement.

Leadership behaviors are important because they are the objective actions the leader takes that impact organizational success. We have all seen brilliant leaders behave in a manner that damages their organization, and we have seen other leaders continually behave in ways that promote ongoing organizational success. Effective Leadership Behaviors drive organizational success and conversely ineffective Leadership Behaviors drive organizational dysfunction or failure.

We use the **Leadership Circle Profile** (LCP) and the associated framework from The Leadership Circle® to explore Leadership Behaviors. The Leadership Circle® Profile is an assessment tool that collects feedback from the leader's boss, boss's boss, peers, and subordinates to provide a 360-degree perspective of the leader's performance along with the leader's self-assessment. The LCP is a unique competency-based 360-degree assessment and includes belief systems and assumptions that underpin a leader's behavior. This tool integrates well with other tools, such as the Enneagram leadership type model and MAP Developmental Perspective model in a way that provides great insight to leaders.

Figure 4.3 Sample LCP Feedback

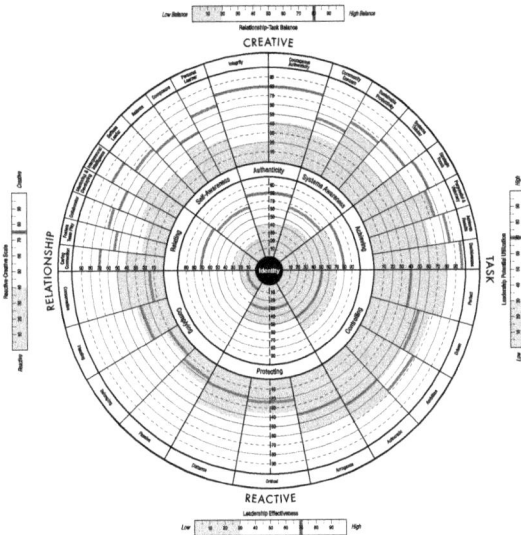

In looking at this simple example of feedback, you will notice that the graph shows high scores in both task creative and task reactive areas (more gray on the right side). From this part of the score we can tell that others perceive this leader as more task-focused than people-focused. This score may be appropriate for the job or this leader may learn from the assessment that he is not giving enough attention to people-related components of leadership. An additional piece of information is also important: above the gray shading, you will see a line which reflects how the leader self-scored. The leader sees his behavior differently than peers see him. This difference could be an inaccurate self-perception; it is important that leaders have an accurate view of what others see to be able to make appropriate changes and gauge the impact of these changes. This tool not only allows you to identify possible behavioral changes, it can also help you improve your self-awareness, specifically by understanding how others see you. It is this ability to see what others see that will allow you to target your behavioral changes and fine-tune your effectiveness.

In addition to understanding your own Leadership Behaviors, there is great value in exploring the teams' (steering committee and program team) behaviors. The LCP assessment results can be combined to create a team profile, which can help a leader understand how he behaves compared to the team norms. As the leader of the entire group, you will be able to identify strengths and risks based on the composite behavior. You can also map the team behaviors to the culture and identify disconnects. This information can feed into an individual and also a team development plan and process.

Organizational culture is measured by asking leaders their views on key organizational indicators. We use a tool created by Metcalf & Associates called the Culture Assessment that looks at 20 organizational measures that capture both elements of business model and the organizational philosophy that serves as the foundation for culture. This assessment uses a one to five scale for each of the measures to evaluate organizational beliefs (often reflected in organizational behaviors). We work with the leadership team to identify where the organization is at the start and where they need to be to support implementation success. The following is a subset of the elements you would evaluate:

Table 4.2

Vision and strategic direction	Customer service
Growth funding	Quality
Decision making	Bias for improvement
Capacity for change	Standardization
Accountability	Centralization
Technology	Communication
Innovation	Resource alignment

The assessment process involves each leader giving his view of the current state and the goal state of the culture indicators. This process is interesting in the range of responses leadership teams often provide, and identifies gaps not only between current and goal state, but also the gaps between key leaders within the organization. When assessment results are highly divergent, the assessment process results in facilitated discussions to help leaders begin to come together as a team and create a shared view of where they are going and how they will proceed. This tool can be tailored to specific organizations and is not statistically validated. The purpose of this activity is to create a shared understanding across the team of the current state, future state, and gap to be addressed.

The culture results can also be mapped to the team LCP group scores to identify areas where their observed behavior is not consistent with the culture they are trying to create.

Organization Systems and Processes – This is the area where most change programs focus, looking at the current organization through several lenses (as reflected in Table 4.1 Assessment Overview). Because entire books are written that provide these tools, we will provide a few examples of the items listed in the table. Most organizations taking on major change initiatives either are working with an internal or external consulting firm that has a well-developed assessment methodology. The assessment names and contents vary slightly, but tend to cover approximately the same content.

Stakeholder Impact

Stakeholders are people who will be directly or indirectly impacted by the change. We will use this information as the basis for additional data collection to define stakeholder expectations as well as a detailed implementation plan. Interviewing stakeholders is your first opportunity to begin engaging them and building commitment to the program. Your goal is more than just gathering information—it is gaining support.

Leaders occasionally overlook the board as they consider stakeholder input. It is important to gather board input for large scale programs that require significant investments. This is another opportunity to build support and excitement for the initiatives you are taking to accomplish the organization's strategy.

Table 4.3: Stakeholder Impact Analysis

Stakeholder name (Group)	Who to interview	Impact of change	Perception of change	Role supporting change	Level of commitment (h, m, l)

User Impact Analysis

Users are people whose jobs will be directly impacted by the change; they are a subset of the stakeholder group and may also be called "change targets" in some change management approaches, because they are the ones whose jobs change. We will use this information as the foundation for communication planning, job change discussions, training, coaching plan, and staffing discussions. This assessment is critical to successfully manage human performance risk (the system works, but people do not know how to use it). Again, by engaging users early you begin building support among important constituent groups. This is an opportunity to gather their input and beginning generating support and excitement about the program and their involvement in it.

> By engaging users early you begin building support among important constituent groups.

Table 4.4: User Impact Analysis

Function / process	Process / people changes	New skills	Position changes

Change Initiative Inventory

Most organizations are concurrently engaged in several change initiatives. To ensure that programs are successful, it is critical that people are getting clear and consistent messages about changes, how they interconnect, and their impact. Additionally, people have a "change capacity" that gauges how much change they are able to absorb and remain productive. We also have an energy capacity and it is important to manage the amount of energy we expect people to expend. We can go into a deficit zone for a short period of time, but this is not sustainable. If people spend too much time in deficit before the program is implemented, your program implementation could be at risk. By managing the change volume and human energy, you reduce the risk of diverting attention and focus and sub-optimizing program results.

> To ensure that programs are successful, it is critical that people are getting clear and consistent messages about changes, how they interconnect, and their impact.

Table 4.5: Change Initiative Inventory

Change initiative	Description	Who impacted (user groups / plants)	How does it impact other initiatives?	Timing

Document Current Process Flow and Potential Changes

One of the highest impact activities that can happen during the assessment phase is to map the end-to-end process flow for the change. There are several helpful approaches to mapping process that range from the simple to complex and in some industries there are government standards regulating these process flows. A process flow chart or map indicates from start to finish the steps to successfully accomplish the process. This process flow should include all major process steps organized in "swim lanes," or by job responsibility. Additionally, it should include inputs, outputs, deliverables, and process measures. These process flows can be quite detailed if you are incorporating analytics into a large-scale change, such as an enterprise software implementation. Your program manager will have a clear understanding of what is standard for your industry. As a reference, we provide a sample flow chart of the generic organizational transformation process in the sample section later in the chapter.

> One of the highest impact activities that can happen during the assessment phase is to map the end-to-end process flow for the change.

After you have documented the current process, identify key areas impacted by the change. This document can help you identify areas with the greatest change and inform how you time-phase the changes.

As an example, for incorporating predictive analytics into the sales process and toolkit, we discovered that the sales team would have the largest volume of job change on day one of implementation as they would be changing territory focus, sales call preparation and information used during the sales call. Because we identified the change in advance, we actually implemented job changes in advance using a paper version and incorporated sales force feedback so that the day the system went live, they were only dealing with an automated system for a familiar job. This type of user impact becomes much clearer when you look at a range of assessments simultaneously.

It is helpful to leverage multiple assessments at the same time to paint a more complete and accurate picture of the broad range of change, the impact it will have on various groups, and also the risks associated with that impact. Keep in mind that interpreting the data from these and other assessments may require specialized expertise. Similar to getting medical tests, the potential value of the information is only realized with proper translation. To that end, having a subject matter expert interpret the series of assessments as the foundation for your development plan can significantly increase your results since you will know exactly where to focus your efforts.

Now that we have presented four different types of assessments, you will have the opportunity to select the ones you are moved to take and consider how best to utilize the results.

Stories and Examples

Our leader, George, is a big fan of assessments. He conducted several of them to get a solid picture of his current leadership capacity, as well as that of his key leaders on the steering committee and program team. Beyond the leader assessments, he also assessed the organization's culture and conducted several assessments on systems and processes. He will describe his assessment process in the following section.

Leader individual and team assessments

I am an Enneagram type seven (enthusiast) and developmentally a Strategist. I am well positioned to lead or play a significant role on the program team. I also asked that the other steering committee members get assessed using the Enneagram and the MAP. I also took the DEV:Q™ and realize that I am considered Principal (refer to the image of assessments earlier in this chapter). I learned that the steering committee type was also enthusiast with a second high score of challenger. This group is highly focused on initiating activities and getting results. They do not have a high representation from the other process types called cooperators or soloists (These Enneagram process types can be found in the Innovative Leaders Guide to Transforming Organizations Chapter One for further information.). This is important information for us to have going forward. It is important to note that programs will be most successful when all of the types are represented.

On the Developmental Perspective assessment (MAP), we learned the range is Achiever to Strategist (See Innovative Leaders Guide to Transforming Organizations in Chapter Two for definition of levels.). This is a reasonable range for a leadership team. It will be important for us to develop working norms that support success for people at all levels. As a team, we will also need to understand that the norms within the steering committee will be different than norms when collaborating with other people and teams. Many people on the program team will be functioning at the expert Developmental Perspective and will have a very different approach for interaction.

On the DEV:Q™, the team average was a 36, which means that the team is heavily focused on being efficient and effective, and they tend to focus on analytics and deployment. This is a great profile for the implementation team, and we need to make sure that there is also an emphasis on the more strategic tasks on the steering committee. Since my scores show I tend to perform at a 45 or principal level, I will fulfill the tasks of creating synergy across programs as well as alignment between all of the parts within the program.

I also encouraged the team to take the LCP and combined the results to look at the collective group. What I learned was that the steering committee is more results-oriented than people-oriented. This orientation made the company very successful in a rather steady state environment. As we embark on a phase where the organization will be implementing significant transformational change, the steering committee will need to be aware of our tendency to preference results over people. We will need to resist this "habit" and take the time necessary to coach and mentor people through the many transitions they will face over the next 18 to 24 months.

Culture

To better understand the culture change necessary, the ten person steering committee completed the culture assessment. We found that there were a broad range of responses among the group to some of the measures. We worked with a facilitator to better understand our differences and build agreement among our own steering committee with regard to the current situation and what we want going forward. It's important to note that the objective wasn't to reach a consensus, but to find a shared understanding of perspectives. While it took a long time, this was a helpful exercise for me personally, as it helped me understand the broad range of views we have simply on the steering committee. We do not see the world in the same way, so we will need to check our assumptions often. I assumed others would make decisions similar to mine, and that is clearly not true. We will need to discuss our decisions much more than I anticipated to ensure that everyone is on the same page.

The following chart indicates the largest gaps in where we are now and where we want to be. The next step is to identify what needs to be addressed and over what timeframe. We determined as a group that our top needs for successful change are to improve employee capacity to change and innovation. Unless these are addressed quickly, the risk associated with the change will be very high. Directly after that is career and employee development. Our perception of what is necessary is really out of balance. We will need to continue to look for more effective ways to let people know what to expect throughout the implementation. The scores in this area indicate a lack of understanding of what is necessary.

Figure 4.4: Organizational Health Check

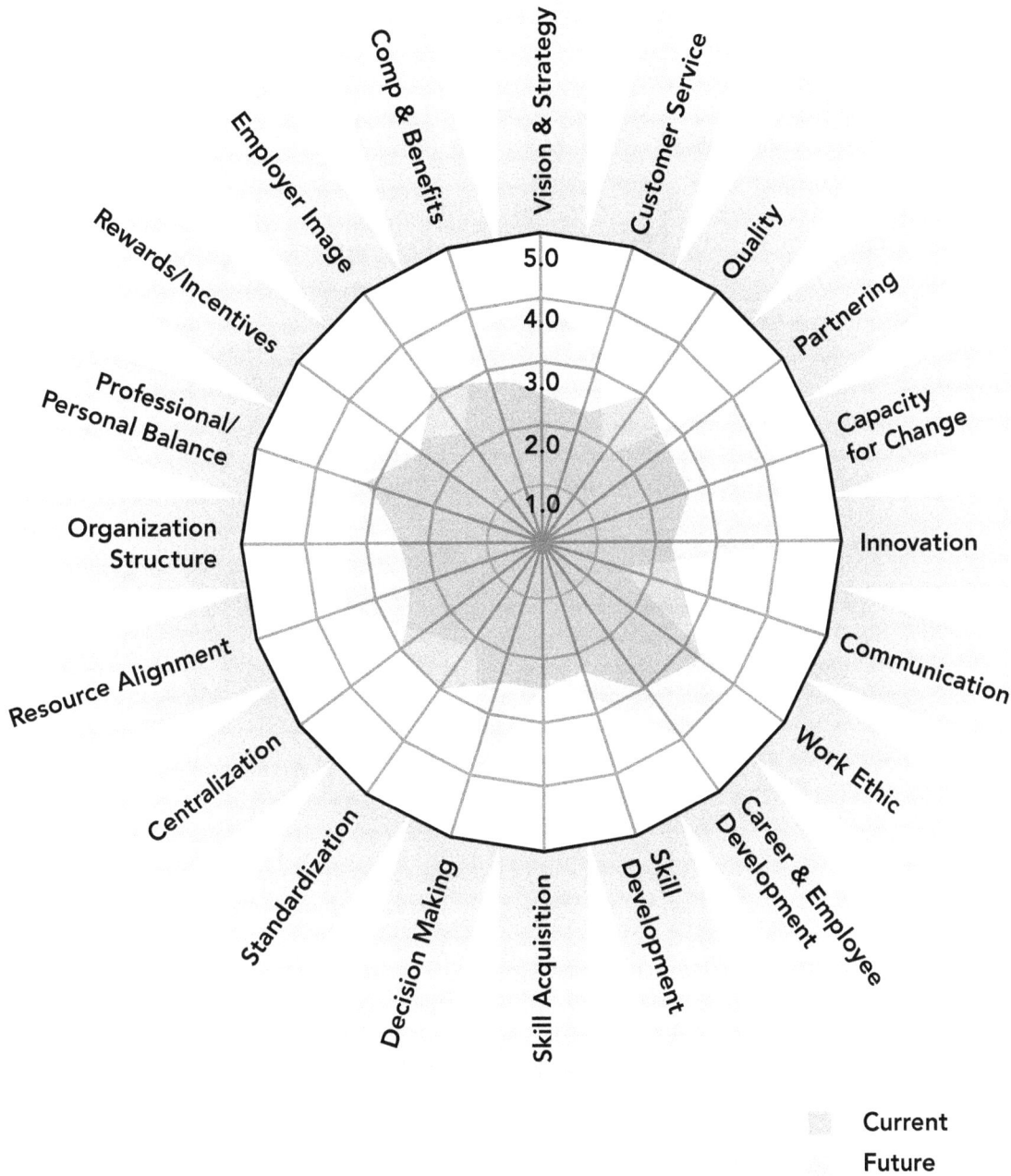

Current
Future

Systems and Processes

As shown in Figure 4.4 above, systems and processes generally get all of the attention with regard to assessments, so we will not spend as much time here because this is the area most leaders already have a handle on. The one assessment we are including below is the User Impact Assessment. It is important to understand user impact by group as the foundation for implementation planning and also hiring, communication, job change discussions, and several other areas.

Table 4.6: User Impact Assessment

Function / process	Process / people changes	New skills	Position changes
IT Data modeling and data integration	New data modeling skills to support analytics will be required. Additionally, the Extract Transform and Load (ETL) techniques differ from traditional transactional programming. The use of unstructured data (e.g., articles, documents, e-mail, and blogs) will require Hadoop to mine the text for analysis. If social media will be mined, social media streams will need to be acquired and software configured to extract the contents.	Dimensional data modeling Large data volume ETL processing Social media sentiment analysis	Additional skills and responsibilities for data architects Additional programmers for ETL Additional programmers for Hadoop Social media analysts
Predictive analytic modeling	Data scientists will consume the data from the integrated data warehouse to conduct segment and regression analysis. As attributes are identified that correlate with a business outcome, models will be developed, refined, validated, and trained.	Large volume data and statistical analysis	Data scientists
Visual reporting via dashboards	Large volume data and complex statistical models are easier to understand with interactive visualizations. The measures, dimensions, and hierarchy values are established by the business users. The data volume, complexity, and need to interact with supporting details will determine the most effective visual elements. Negotiation may be necessary to ensure fast response times and a comprehensible user experience.	Data analysis and user interface design for analytics	Data analysts User experience designers Business Intelligence developers
Contract financial analysis	Contract analysis will require new Key Performance Indicators (KPI's), which need to be defined and validated. The process to acquire the data will be substantially simplified through the use of the data warehouse and business intelligence interfaces.	Skills will be upgraded to transition from data acquisition to metric definition and financial analysis	Financial analysts
Contract performance review	Contract performance will be significantly more data and metric driven. Performance across geographies and customer comparisons will become the new norm during reviews. Recommendations for improvements will be supported with data, predictive models and forecasts for multiple scenarios.	Financial forecasting and scenario analysts	Financial analyst
Contract negotiation	Contract negotiation with customers will be significantly more data driven, with a focus on past performance metrics and market segment utilization. As contract parameter changes are discussed, scenarios will be compared with performance metrics to ensure all parties meet their objects.	Data-driven presentation skills Scenario analysis	Additional training for the current sales force

To help plan the transformation, it was critical to start with a consistent understanding of our current processes and information used to support the organization. The entire contract review and negotiation processes were mapped using swim lanes to emphasize hand-offs between teams. We also used differently colored blocks to indicate which systems are used by the different tasks. As the chart grew, it was an awakening moment for the teams to understand how complex and inefficient the processes became. It was also apparent that the team was highly dependent on a collection of spreadsheets that were duplicative and only understood by a few individuals. The consolidated process map also helped the technical team understand where information was used and enabled them to recommend options to structure it to meet multiple needs.

With a thorough understanding of the current state, the team was prepared to draft the future processes. The transition from "as is" to "to be" energized the team as they brainstormed how to overcome years of frustration from manual processes, lack of information, and poorly integrated systems. This also helped them start to envision their alignment with future roles.

A key element of the process map exercise was to separate the underlying problems from individuals and transfer the problems to the map. Essentially, it became a common "enemy" that the teams could focus on rather than each other or specific individuals. By participating in mapping and review sessions, the leadership team could also assess the involvement of individuals to assess their willingness to raise questions, make recommendations, embrace change, and monitor progress.

> To help plan the transformation, it was critical to start with a consistent understanding of our current processes and information used to support the organization.

As the process map and program team member assessments evolved, the team was able to start crafting a transformation roadmap based on all elements that were "in motion." As the number of impacted systems, interfaces, sub-processes, skills, and teams were identified, the team could assess the magnitude of the change and start defining how they could coordinate all elements of the change. There was a desire to use a standard model to facilitate the transformation. Through extensive discussions, the team realized they could reference general models to ensure they weren't missing elements, but the transformation model must be specific to our organization, processes and challenges.

As a leader, it was vital that I participate, but not direct the outcome. I had to maintain focus on guiding the team while allowing them time to discover, reflect, brainstorm, and refine their recommendations. This ensured their ownership of the transformation and outcome.

Because of the size of the charts (12-foot long wall chart with 9-point font), it is not included in this document. We did, however, provide the process chart we used for transforming organizations. This is not organized by role of person performing the task, but rather by major activity to be performed over time. We realize the image is small—this is included as an example, not as a guide. You will create your own process flows based on your specific implementation that could include such items as: roles of people performing the tasks, deliverables, hand-offs, measures, and risks.

The data we collected during this phase was used to update prior documents such as the change foundation document and even caused slight modifications to the charter. It was also the foundation for several plans we created.

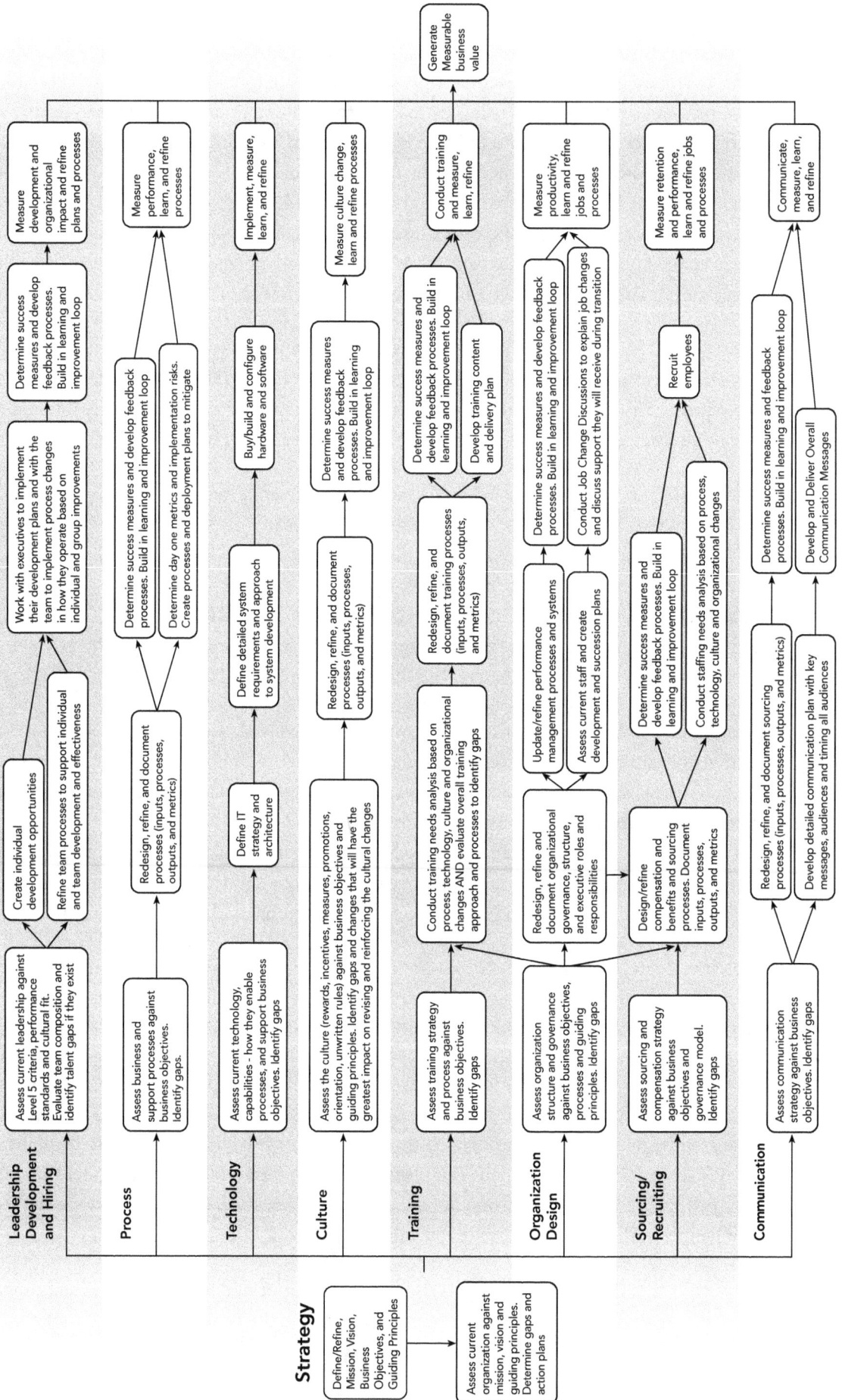

Table 4.7

Organizational Transformation Model

Strategy
- Define/Refine, Mission, Vision, Business Objectives, and Guiding Principles
- Assess current organization against mission, vision and guiding principles. Determine gaps and action plans

Leadership Development and Hiring
- Assess current leadership against Level 5 criteria, performance standards and cultural fit. Evaluate team composition and identify talent gaps if they exist
- Create individual development opportunities
- Refine team processes to support individual and team development and effectiveness
- Work with executives to implement their development plans and with the team to implement process changes in how they operate based on individual and group improvements
- Determine success measures and develop feedback processes. Build in learning and improvement loop
- Measure development and organizational impact and refine plans and processes

Process
- Assess business and support processes against business objectives. Identify gaps.
- Redesign, refine, and document processes (inputs, processes, outputs, and metrics)
- Determine success measures and develop feedback processes. Build in learning and improvement loop
- Determine day one metrics and implementation risks. Create processes and deployment plans to mitigate
- Measure performance, learn, and refine processes

Technology
- Assess current technology, capabilities - how they enable processes, and support business objectives. Identify gaps
- Define IT strategy and architecture
- Define detailed system requirements and approach to system development
- Buy/build and configure hardware and software
- Implement, measure, learn, and refine

Culture
- Assess the culture (rewards, incentives, measures, promotions, orientation, unwritten rules) against business objectives and guiding principles. Identify gaps and changes that will have the greatest impact on revising and reinforcing the cultural changes
- Redesign, refine, and document processes (inputs, processes, outputs, and metrics)
- Determine success measures and develop feedback processes. Build in learning and improvement loop
- Measure culture change, learn and refine processes

Training
- Assess training strategy and process against business objectives. Identify gaps
- Conduct training needs analysis based on process, technology, culture and organizational changes AND evaluate overall training approach and processes to identify gaps
- Redesign, refine, and document training processes (inputs, processes, outputs, and metrics)
- Determine success measures and develop feedback processes. Build in learning and improvement loop
- Develop training content and delivery plan
- Conduct training and measure, learn, refine

Organization Design
- Assess organization structure and governance against business objectives, processes and guiding principles. Identify gaps
- Redesign, refine and document organizational governance, structure, and executive roles and responsibilities
- Update/refine performance management processes and systems
- Assess current staff and create development and succession plans
- Determine success measures and develop feedback processes. Build in learning and improvement loop
- Conduct Job Change Discussions to explain job changes and discuss support they will receive during transition
- Measure productivity, learn and refine jobs and processes

Sourcing/Recruiting
- Assess sourcing and compensation strategy against business objectives and governance model. Identify gaps
- Design/refine compensation and benefits and sourcing processes. Document inputs, processes, outputs, and metrics
- Conduct staffing needs analysis based on process, technology, culture and organizational changes
- Determine success measures and develop feedback processes. Build in learning and improvement loop
- Recruit employees
- Measure retention and performance, learn and refine jobs and processes

Communication
- Assess communication strategy against business objectives. Identify gaps
- Redesign, refine, and document sourcing processes (inputs, processes, outputs, and metrics)
- Develop detailed communication plan with key messages, audiences and timing all audiences
- Determine success measures and feedback processes. Build in learning and improvement loop
- Develop and Deliver Overall Communication Messages
- Communicate, measure, learn, and refine

Generate Measurable business value

Innovative Leadership Reflection Questions

To help you develop your action plan, it is time to further clarify your direction using reflection questions. These questions are organized to reflect the four native domains introduced in Section I. As a reminder, this is an opportunity to practice Innovative Leadership with consideration of how your change plan will affect changes in your intentions, actions, culture, and systems. These questions are arranged to help you explore each of these domains. The questions for "What do I think/believe" reflect your intentions. The questions "What do I do?" reflect your actions. The questions "What do we believe?" reflect culture. The questions "How do we do this?" reflect systems. This exercise was designed to help you start practicing Innovative Leadership as you analyze your situation and strengths.

As a reminder, the table contains several questions for each domain and is applicable to a broad range of programs. We recommend you choose two to four questions from each domain that best apply to your specific situation.

Table 4.8

QUESTIONS TO GUIDE THE LEADER AND ORGANIZATION

What do I think / believe?
- Do I need to change to accomplish my goals? Is the change in perspective or expanded capability at the same level?
- What Developmental Perspective do I think reflects my center of gravity? How will that impact success in my leadership role?
- What level do I think is required for me to perform my job effectively now? In the future?
- How satisfied am I with my performance toward my goals?
- Am I able to balance business and personal commitments? How does my leadership style impact my ability to meet my overall life goals?
- Notice my own interpretation of the urgency of the change and what it means for me personally. What will need to change for me to be the leader I aspire to be?
- How has my leadership style contributed to the organization's success? Have I done things that did not produce the results I had hoped? How would I change to produce different results?
- How would I like to impact the people who work for me? Have they grown and met their career goals while working for me? What have they contributed to the organization while working for me?
- If I am leading a change initiative, what will I need to change to lead this effort effectively? Will I lead the same way this time, or will I change from what I did in the past?

What do I do?
- What assessments am I taking to gather objective data about my performance? This could include performance appraisals, developmental assessments, 360° feedback, or informal feedback from multiple sources. What actions will I take based on what I learned from these assessments?
- How do I model appropriate responses to the sense of urgency in personal actions that are true for me while supporting the organizational objectives?
- How do I use the assessment process to begin building involvement, excitement, and commitment for the program?
- How do I balance my desire to gather data with my requirement to deliver results quickly?
- Have I used the data from all key stakeholders, including our board when appropriate?

What do we believe?

- Are we an organization that believes in assessments and collects data?
- Do we use data to make decisions, or do we prefer intuition or "gut feel"?
- Do we value and trust leadership assessments? Team-oriented assessments?
- Are people willing to share information honestly when you start asking questions about how they do their jobs?
- Are people able to quantify what they do and how they do it?
- Do we understand our current and future culture, and the gaps between?

How do we do this?

- How do we administer the wide range of assessments? Do we have standard tools we would like to use?
- If we collect data for this program, do we want to take time to identify leading indicators to measure going forward, or is this just one-time data collection to help us understand what we need to learn to run the program?
- Can we leverage data we already collect through other means?
- Who will see the data and how will they use it? Are there any concerns that if we share the data it could have an impact on our competitive position?
- What systems and processes are enablers and barriers that will impact my development?
- What processes and measures alert us to urgency in our system that we need to tend to? What are the early warning signs?
- What processes measure your progress? Are you progressing as measured by criteria that will increase your professional effectiveness? Are you progressing against your personal standards? How will your support system or organization reward or punish your changes based on the measures?
- Do the measures indicate a sense of urgency to you that support focusing on development?

Now that George has completed the assessments, it is time to take a look at the reflection questions. He will think through how to use the data he gathered to influence his next steps.

What do I think/believe?

- ***What Developmental Perspective (DEV:Q™ or MAP assessment results) do you think reflects your center of gravity? How will that impact your success in your leadership role?***

  During the assessment phase, I learned that the team's center of gravity is that of analyst with a task orientation focused on efficiency and effectiveness.

  I also learned that I am a Strategist using the MAP assessment and a 45 using the DEV:Q™ assessment. This Developmental Perspective will help me play an important strategic role in the success of this program. I also learned that because of my Developmental Perspective, I have different working and communication styles than others. I am coming to realize that I will need to be deliberate about what and how I communicate with those on the steering committee and even more careful with how I communicate to others outside of the team. I have a tendency to speak over people's heads, or give more information than they want or need from me. It is a tough realization that if I communicate with people the way I want them to communicate with me, I may actually be causing performance problems. This makes me think I need to be more aware.

■ *If I am leading a change initiative, what will I need to change to lead this effort effectively? Will I lead the same way this time, or will I change from what I did in the past?*

Through the assessments and coaching, I've realized that any single style won't succeed in all situations or transformations. I need to be extremely conscious of the situation and participants to adjust my approach. I frequently envision a multidimensional model that balances the team's foundational understanding, need for deeper analysis, desired outcome, and expectation for their participation. I try to preplan most situations so I can adjust my behavior and responses to meet their needs relative to the desired outcome. I've found it important to avoid jumping to conclusions or driving for an outcome that they won't support in the medium- to long-term. That approach needs to be balanced with a "that train already left the station" approach to prevent analysis paralysis or continuous analysis of the strategy. I am careful to use cliché statements like this sparingly, but there are times it is important to ensure people understand we are moving with aggressive deadlines and any individual delay will have an adverse impact on the overall program success.

I have also realized that I'll need to be more creative to assessing our skill development. I'm leading the implementation of quantitative skills that I don't possess nor know how to measure. I'll need to develop trust in external experts and ensure they are training and mentoring our team members. Since we're developing quantitative skills, we'll need to be more subjective in our progress assessments.

What do I do?

■ *How do I model appropriate responses to the sense of urgency in personal actions that are true for me while supporting the organizational objectives?*

Through the use of several assessments (e.g., the DEV:Q™ for an understanding of my orientation and preference, the MAP for Developmental Perspective, and the LCP 360° assessment) to see how others view my behavior, I've realized I need to carefully adjust my communications and actions based on the audience. I've ensured I proactively meet with executive sponsors (frequently one-on-one) and continually reinforce the vision to ensure they're up-to-date and I've incorporated their recommendations. When meeting with the department managers, I've adjusted my style to be more encouraging with more listening, while still coaching them toward an aggressive timeline to realize the benefits. That coaching must be facilitative since they need to completely embrace all of their commitments. To foster open communications and connections with the operational staff, I've leveraged a communication plan that mixes published documentation (e.g., newsletters, blogs, and status reports) and "town hall" sessions to cultivate approachability. For many operational staff members, the continuous communications and approachability convey the importance and drive behind the transformation.

The other element that strikes me about my assessment results is that I am much more comfortable with big picture and ambiguity, where others want more structure and certainty. I work hard to meet them where they are and provide clear and specific answers to their questions rather than suggesting that they have the skills to figure things out. I am finding that everyone's anxiety decreases when I remember to provide more detailed answers to questions than I traditionally do.

■ *How do I balance my desire to gather data with my requirement to deliver results quickly?*

This has been one of the more difficult parts of the analytics transformation. The traditional "Waterfall" delivery method can be a recipe for disaster with analytics. However, that is the delivery method our organization knows, trusts, expects, and requires. By deferring the analysis and benefit realization, the risk is exponentially higher. It is especially easy to lose executive sponsorship if the new approach doesn't deliver some measureable benefits quickly. I've successfully campaigned for a pilot using an Agile delivery methodology. While having all data fully integrated and prepared for broad analysis would be desirable and my preference, waiting for that to happen would likely take years and derail our vision.

With the Agile method, we've been able to prioritize data sources with the highest interest and hypothesized value. Rather than wait for all complementary data sources, we've structured, explored, cleansed, and analyzed each source as fast as possible. As our predictive models have evolved, we've communicated they are fluid and will continue to evolve. By driving for rapid results and frequent revisions, we've reduced risk, realized early benefits (which encourage the entire team), demonstrated success, and ensured our executive sponsors can monitor continual progress.

Beyond the success of the program, the same is true for assessments and perfect data on team members. We're using new approaches and techniques. We've had to accept that not all team members will embrace the transformation at the same pace. The use of assessments has provided tremendous insights, but we need to move forward with partial information, and let each team member demonstrate their own success. Our Agile method has afforded them more opportunities with incremental work and accomplishments. We've had to consider those outcomes as a vital data point as we continue to progress.

> The traditional "Waterfall" delivery method can be a recipe for disaster with analytics.

What do we believe?

■ *Do we use data to make decisions, or do we prefer intuition or "gut feel"?*

We are a very traditional, data-driven firm. Our ability to stay in business is based on the collection and validation of data. The pressure we're facing requires us to ingest data faster and respond more quickly. "Perfect" responses are becoming less likely, and we need to embrace that reality.

The same is true for developing leaders. Assessments are vital to understand an individual's orientation. We'll use that data to avoid "gut" decisions on building teams. We will continue to recognize that team members grow and change with training and coaching. We'll continue to use assessments to validate their growth and refine their development plans. Assessments for entire teams have helped us structure well-balanced teams. Rather than select team members that "play nice together", we're now able to staff based on the situation, balanced perspectives, and complementary orientations.

■ *Do we understand our current and future culture, and the gaps between?*

As part of our transformation, we've had to be very objective on what has worked well in our past and what needs to change to enable our future. Our future needs to be increasingly quantitative with faster responses. Our culture has been very risk averse. It seems the endless collection and analysis of data enables people to defer decisions and actions. For operational decisions, we're remediating the risk aversion by rewarding rapid analysis, quantified recommendations, and action plans with controllable risks. This will enable us to make smaller decisions faster and make small "course corrections" for small errors. This is a significant cultural shift that will require support from all leadership levels.

How do we do this?

■ *How do we administer the wide range of assessments? Do we have standard tools we would like to use?*

To provide a consistent and cost effective baseline for our leaders and teams, we've standardized on a core set of assessments. They include Enneagram, DEV:Q™ and resilience for all key roles; and MAP and LCP for key leadership and steering committee roles. We used the Organizational Health Check (Figure 4.4 earlier in this chapter), and have also used stakeholder analysis, change foundation scorecard, change readiness assessment, and change alignment assessment. We plan to use other tools during the course of the program. This consistency has given us a baseline and common structure to establish balanced teams. It has also provided us with a common communication structure across the leadership team. We did have some resistance from team members that felt they've completed past assessments that should have been adequate (e.g., Myers Briggs, DISC, and Strength-Finder). We've continued to reinforce that current assessment tools don't measure "personality type" but focus on professional orientation.

■ *If we collect data for this program, do we want to take time to identify leading indicators to measure going forward, or is this just one-time data collection to help us understand what we need to learn to run the program?*

For our analytics transformation, we need to embrace the fact that not all data captured and analyzed will be permanent. The construction of predictive models is based on hypothesis validation. We need to accept that not all hypotheses will be valid. The statistical analysis may also prove that some correlations are simply correlations and not "cause-effect" relationships. Where possible, we'll identify leading indicators and incorporate them into operational models. We'll also capture correlated data to use as validation measures and to quantify adjacent business value.

This reflection process is again giving me things to consider as I look at how we develop as an organization going forward and how our culture will impact our success.

Throughout this chapter, we have reviewed assessment tools that will allow you to have a strong understanding of your current state, as well as—in many instances—your future state. This information serves as the foundation for a well-planned change initiative. It is important to assess your current state in all of the key domains to identify gaps that will put your program at risk if not addressed.

We have provided blank worksheets in the appendix for you to use on your analytics program.

What do I do?

How do we do this?

CHAPTER 5
PLAN YOUR JOURNEY

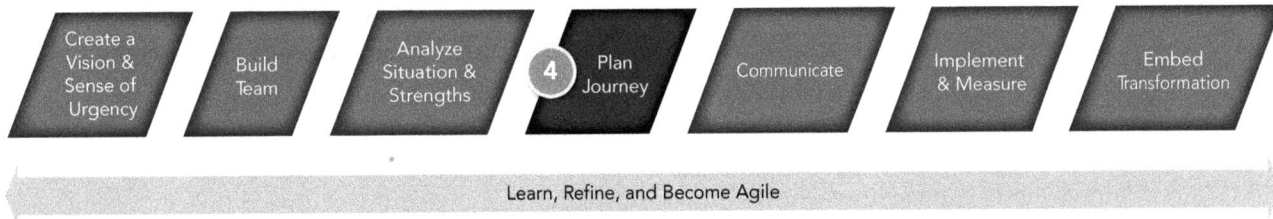

Create a Vision & Sense of Urgency → Build Team → Analyze Situation & Strengths → **4 Plan Journey** → Communicate → Implement & Measure → Embed Transformation

Learn, Refine, and Become Agile

This is the stage in which the program team creates the initial plans that will drive the program forward. The role of the leader is generally to clarify the team's expectations and to answer questions, provide input, and review plans. These early plans will establish the foundation for program performance and success. If plans are not thorough, it will be easy to get off track and later realize that course correction is necessary. **A word of caution at this phase: leaders often want to skip, rush through, or minimize this process.** They want to see results and can become frustrated at the amount of time and money they are spending on plan development.

However, it is often a weak plan that causes a program to fail. One of the six effective tactics in implementing successful transformation is to launch large-scale collaborative planning efforts. This collaboration began in the assessment phase when you asked stakeholders at all levels for their input. It will be important to continue to look for opportunities to solicit input on the plan from all groups impacted by the change and, at the same time, do so in a manner that is efficient.

In addition to supporting the planning process at this phase, leaders will be communicating key messages to promote awareness. While the seven step process addresses communication in the next chapter, in reality, communication begins during the vision creation phase and continues through the entire program. Leaders will increase team effectiveness during times of uncertainty by sharing personal or team stories of triumph to instill a sense of confidence that the right steps are being taken and that the program will succeed.

As the team creates plans, it will be important to pay attention to how often results are delivered. We previously mentioned the idea of making process changes earlier in the program, implementing software later in the program, and demonstrating progress during the analysis stage. This is important not only to manage the volume of impact on users, but also to keep people motivated. It is tough for team members to maintain a sense of urgency when they do not have a deliverable for a year or more. By time phasing results and making them visible to the organization, it is easier to engage team members and those who are picking up roles vacated by people who are "temporarily assigned" to the program.

Just as your assessment looked at the four key domains, your will also use the results of your assessment and gap analysis to create plans that account for gaps in each of the four areas. You will likely have multiple plans (projects) that are synthesized into an overall plan (program). The size and complexity of your plans will depend entirely on the size and complexity of the transformation you are trying to implement. Some program plans can be hundreds of pages and highly complex. The templates and samples we provide in this chapter will be much simpler in nature. If you are doing a program that requires very complex implementation plans, we highly recommend you work with people who are trained and certified in program management and have extensive experience.

> Just as your assessment looked at the four key domains, your will also use the results of your assessment and gap analysis to create plans that account for gaps in each of the four areas.

The table below provides examples of how assessment data can be used as the foundation for specific plans. These individual plans will likely then be consolidated into an overall program plan that is managed by a person or team to track progress, budgets, resource needs, vendors, manage task interconnections and interdependencies, identify risks, and manage key decisions and changes.

Table 5.1

TRANSFORMATION ASSESSMENT OVERVIEW

Leader Mindset – Am I able to successfully lead a complex change? Does my developmental perspective match with program responsibilities?

- Using the MAP Assessment and personality type assessment, identify leader and team development goals. Create development plans

Recommended Tool: MAP Assessment

Leader Behavior – How do my actions impact the program success? Do my Leadership Behaviors align with program requirements?

- Use results of resilience assessment and LCP or other 360° Assessment and create individual and team development plan

Recommended Tool: Resilience Assessment and LCP 360° Assessment

Organizational Culture – How does our culture support and inhibit program success?

Using the Metcalf & Associates Culture Assessment (or others), determine current and future state, identify gaps, and create a culture change plan. You can augment this analysis by evaluating LCP 360° results, if you used that assessment, and have the overall results consolidated

What systems, procedures, and processes do we need to put in place to ensure success?

- Evaluate business performance using clearly established metrics and process owners
- Provide consequences (positive and negative) for performance
- Evaluate the organizational structure and determine what is necessary to support the desired program outcomes and fit within future organizational norms
- Conduct Team Effectiveness Assessment to determine process and organizational system changes that will support program success
- Evaluate organization's readiness to adapt to change
- Evaluate current communication tools and frequency as foundation for program communication plan

- Assess job changes on key roles including task change and workload changes
- Determine risk of the change initiative on the business; identify items such as "day 1" risks as well as program risks
- Technology tools assessment to identify what technological tools you will need to acquire to facilitate the change initiative

Recommended Tools –
- *Existing Business Scorecard*
- *Team Effectiveness Assessment*
- *Change Readiness Assessment*
- *Risk Assessment*
- *Communication Survey*
- *Quality Assessment*
- *Change Readiness Assessment*
- *Technology Tools Assessment*
- *Stakeholder Impact*
- *Change History*
- *Change Initiative Inventory*
- *User Impact Assessment*
- *Stakeholder Impact Assessment*
- *Change Foundation Scorecard*

As you review the assessment results you compiled during the assessment phase, it is now time to determine where to take action. You can start with the leader assessments for both individual and team effectiveness. We have provided several templates below that will support your development planning.

For the individual leader, you may want to use the Leader Development Worksheet, Table 5.2, to identify the impact of specific behaviors on individual and team success. We recommend that you present individual and team results, and then ask each leader to consider the top three areas for improvement and complete the worksheet for each of them. Given the time and energy leaders will spend on the program, the highest priority is to identify any behaviors that will derail the leader, the team, or the program. As George mentioned, a tendency to overwork and become exhausted and short-tempered must be addressed as it will have an adverse impact on the program. Part of the goal with the planning process is to identify significant barriers or threats that need to be addressed during the program. Development requires an investment of time and energy. It is important to have a clear understanding of what will be required of leaders during the program and how their development is included in the investments they are making on the program.

> Given the time and energy leaders will spend on the program, the highest priority is to identify any behaviors that will derail the leader, the team, or the program.

Table 5.2

LEADER DEVELOPMENT WORKSHEET — INPUT TO DEVELOPMENT			
Evaluate and Select Behavioral Change Priorities — Worksheet			
Key Actions	**Detailed Action Planning**	**Skill 1**	**Skill 2**
Select behaviors	Which behaviors do I want to improve or change? Which behaviors do I perform well that I would like to enhance?		
What are the consequences of this behavior?	What will happen if I continue to demonstrate this behavior in the future? How does this behavior impact my customers? How does it impact my career? How are my colleagues impacted? How is my organization impacted?		
Why do I demonstrate this behavior?	I have developed behaviors over the course of my life because they make sense. What has changed that now makes this behavior ineffective?		
How would I like to perform in the future?	Write an end-result statement describing the changes I will make and the impact of those changes. What will an observer see when I have made this change?		
Who will help me change?	Who could I ask to provide me with feedback on how I am doing? Who would be a good mentor?		
What type of support do I want?	Make an agreement with a person I trust about how we would like to support one another in changing behaviors. How will that person hold me accountable for taking this step? How will I support them in changing their behavior? Is there a group that will support me long term?		
What will I do or not do?	What other actions could I take? What am I willing to commit to doing? What am I committed to stopping?		
When will I complete actions?	When will I have completed action items?		

The next template was designed to synthesize development activities reflected in the prior worksheets. Using the information from all of the provided assessments and worksheets, you are now ready to complete your Development Planning Worksheet. This worksheet should reflect the synthesis of your data gathering and personal reflection; it will serve as the foundation for the actions you will take to accomplish your goals. As you define your goals, consider making them SMART goals as defined by the following:

- **Specific** – A specific goal has a much greater chance of being accomplished than a general goal.

- **Measurable** – Establish concrete criteria for measuring progress toward the attainment of each goal you set.

- **Attainable** – When you identify goals that are most important to you, you begin to figure out ways you can make them come true. You develop the attitudes, abilities, skills, and financial capacity to reach them. You begin seeing previously overlooked opportunities to bring yourself closer to the achievement of your goals.

- **Realistic** – To be realistic, a goal must represent an objective toward which you are both willing and able to work toward. A goal can be both high and realistic. You are the only one who can decide the height of your goal; however, be sure that each goal represents substantial progress.

- **Timely** – A goal should be grounded within an approximate time frame. Goals lacking time frames also lack urgency.

Table 5.3

DEVELOPMENT PLANNING WORKSHEET				
Current State	Future State / Goal	Actions	By When?	Measure How do you know?

Now we will take a look at George's development plan based on his assessment results. He focuses on his low resilience scores, and using the Leadership Circle 360° feedback, his behaviors were high on the creative and low on the reactive scales. While his scores were good, he still wants to improve them. He believes these two specific areas will have the most significant impact on the program if not addressed.

Table 5.4

DEVELOPMENT PLANNING WORKSHEET – GEORGE'S EXAMPLE				
Current State	**Future State / Goal**	**Actions**	**By When?**	**Measure - How do you know?**
Leadership behaviors enhance proactive behaviors (less reactive)	Increase effectiveness by modifying my Leadership Behaviors as defined in LCP assessment. - Clearly spell out vision and build engagement among the team and build on systems thinking (enhance understanding of interconnections of all elements within the system) - Coach and develop staff rather than telling them what to do	1. Modify my behaviors by building team engagement for vision and change agenda 2. Get regular feedback from select team members 3. Evaluate my progress with coach weekly 4. Get involved in key elements of the change process that relate to process mapping to develop a stronger systems awareness within our business and also across businesses in our industry	Focus on these actions for the following year	Team feedback; team is growing and requires less intervention; fewer crises
Lack resilience in the areas of maintaining physical well-being and managing thinking	Maintain health and sense of composure during high stress times	5. Mindfulness based stress reduction 6. Exercise regularly 7. Mental focusing activities	Focus on these actions for the next six months	Increased sense of overall well-being and composure under stress Re-assess using previous metrics

Culture Action Plan

The actions resulting from the culture assessment can be integrated into the overall program plan, or be part of the overall program plan. If the program is large enough to have a centralized program management function, we highly recommend integrating all plans into the central one so task interdependencies and staffing requirements can be identified. The larger and more complex the program, the more important it is to understand all of the activities involved. If you do plan the culture change as a separate document, you may want to use a template like the one included in Table 5.5 that indicates the steps to accomplish, who, when, and measures.

Table 5.5: Culture Action Plan

Cultural Imperative	Action to Accomplish	Who	When	Measure (SMART)	Status	Dependency
Innovation	Creative problem solving workshop	Director, Human Resources	Y1, Q2	Demonstrate 10 techniques to boost creative problem solving to the contract analysis team by the end of Q2	Open	None
Decision making	Demonstrate empowerment decision matrix	Director, Contract Analysis	Y1, Q3	Demonstrate 5 quantitative measures with outcome matrix to empower the contract analysis by the end of Q3	Open	None

System and Process Planning

Most large complex programs are run by people with expertise in creating program plans and who are certified using standard tools and processes through organizations like Project Management Institute (PMI). As the leader, it is not likely you will be deeply involved in creating the plan, rather, you will need to have a reasonable level of confidence that the plan—as built—will deliver the outcomes you expect. You will likely be using reports like the following to track results. These program management spreadsheets or programs may have several thousand tasks, so you may also be reviewing summaries.

> It is often important to time phase the program to demonstrate quick wins.

In addition to planning the activities to complete the program, it is often important to time phase the program to demonstrate quick wins. If you are using an approach like Agile Development for technology programs, you will automatically have an ongoing release schedule that provides quick wins. If you are using a more traditional approach, it is important to attend to the timing of results. Following is an example of one of the many approaches to tracking program tasks, level of effort, and progress toward completion.

Table 5.6

Sprint	Story ID	Story	Release (target)	Estimate	Remaining
8	113	As a contract analyst, I need to see a chart (by product) of the sales volume by month so that I can assess past contract sales volumes	3	12	12
8	125	As a contract analyst, I need to be able to adjust the future growth rate by month so I can project profitability	3	20	20
8	126	As a contract analyst, I need to be able to save a project scenario so that I can revise and present it	3	6	6

In addition to overall program plans, the program will likely have several strategy documents that spell out the approach behind the estimates. The steering committee will likely want to have a clear understanding of the strategy and the associated key decisions that form the foundation of the estimates. You may want to share responsibilities across the team; for example, the HR lead will review communication and training plans, while the CIO will review the technology and disaster recovery plans. It will be important to ensure that the various plans coordinate across the group to verify that all members of the program team are working in conjunction with one another. You may want to encourage discussions early on with the program team to clarify how they will work together, what they will track, and how often they will collaborate.

If you are on the steering committee, you are responsible for program oversight. You will want to ensure the program team has a plan for program oversight, and coordinate with the program team to delineate their roles and yours to ensure proper oversight balanced with granting your team autonomy to accomplish their work. This is frequently accomplished by completing a RACI (Responsible, Accountable, Consulted, and Informed) chart. By completing the chart with major roles (by name) and the expected level of involvement, the team will have complete clarity on involvement expectations. You will want to revisit the charter to ensure that key deliverables and timelines are still correct. You will also want to clarify the level of authority for the program team as well as the level of involvement you want to have. For a large-scale change, it is critical that the steering committee is heavily involved (some more than others) as it is ultimately responsible for the overall impact this program will have on the company. Given your overall role in business oversight, you are the most aware of leading indicators and potential risks. Each steering committee will find their own balance for involvement versus autonomy—that will change based on phase of the program, as well as other factors such as program team maturity over time.

The following chart provides an example of the RACI evaluation for a subset of a task that many organizations may falsely assume is to be solved solely by the IT development team. We provide this to give an example of how this chart might be used to help clarify the expectations between multiple teams. This information then serves as input to determine program staffing levels, timelines, and accountabilities for key deliverables.

Table 5.7: RACI Chart

TASK	Director, Contract Analysis	Manager, Contract Analysis	Data Scientist	IT Development Team
Define contract profitability metrics	A	R	I	I
Develop profitability projection algorithm	I	I	R/A	I
Assess profitability projection utility	A	R	C	
Incorporate profitability projections into contract analysis tool	I	C	C	R/A

Legend:
R = Responsible – person that does the work
A = Accountable – resource who is the final approving authority or ultimately accountable
C = Consulted – those whose opinion and feedback are sought and there is two-way communication with them
I = Informed – those who are kept updated on the progress and with whom there is just one-way communication

As we mentioned at the beginning of this chapter, plans are built on the foundation of work you did in earlier stages. It is important to build on the input you received and continue to gather input from impacted groups on the viability of the plans. Organizations often conduct events such as implementation workshops where they solicit input, prioritize initiatives, identify specific job and role changes, and evaluate risks. This input is then synthesized by members of the program team to ensure that plans are comprehensive, and that participants and stakeholders have been given a voice in the changes that will impact them. This is another opportunity to build commitment early in the change process that pays dividends during implementation.

Innovative Leadership Reflection Questions

To help you develop your action plan, it is time to further clarify your direction using reflection questions. These questions are organized to reflect the four native domains introduced in Section I. As a reminder, this is an opportunity to practice Innovative Leadership by considering how your change plan will affect changes in your intentions, actions, culture, and systems. These questions are arranged to help you explore each of these domains. The questions for "What do I think/believe?" reflect your intentions. The questions "What do I do?" reflect your actions. The questions "What do we believe?" reflect culture. The questions "How do we do this?" reflect systems. Thus, we designed this exercise to help you start practicing Innovative Leadership as you create your vision and define your direction.

The table contains several questions for each domain to be applicable to a broad range of programs. We recommend you choose two to four questions from each domain that best apply to your specific situation.

Table 5.8

QUESTIONS TO GUIDE THE LEADER AND ORGANIZATION

What do I think / believe?
- Do I need to change my perspective or skills to succeed? If so, what changes are necessary?
- How can I benefit from the success of the program?
- What do I consider my personal short-term wins? Program short-term wins? Organizational short-term wins?
- How do we incorporate short-term wins into the program without impacting long-term program success, schedule, or cost?

What do I do?
- How can I effectively develop myself and empower others? How do I support their success and the success of the organization?
- What decisions need to be made in the short-term to support long-term success?
- What wins can I identify and support that solve "problems" for others, or that are seeds for future shifts?
- How will I deliver clear, concise feedback that will empower others to correct, redirect, or recalibrate their behavior and feel motivated to make necessary changes?

- How do I request and deliver clear and concise feedback that allows me to grow and to support the growth of others?
- How do I determine who is ready for change and what additional support may be required for those who are resistant? Is change readiness included in the plan?
- How am I funding programs and acting to increase organizational awareness and commitment?
- What creative solutions can I find to increase organizational awareness?
- How am I following through on pre-established consequences for behaviors that undermine our success during the planning phase?
- How can I respond to undermining conflicts as learning opportunities?
- How do I encourage bad news, as well as good?
- How am I assigning work to ensure the change is accomplished?
- How am I engaging key constituents to ensure their input is considered and that they are involved throughout the process in meaningful ways?

What do we believe?

- Which wins will provide meaningful results in the eyes of the organization? Which will provide the greatest momentum toward stated organizational objectives?
- Which wins will provide emotionally meaningful results?
- Which stories can we tell about the wins that will be shared with the organization in public settings such as town hall meetings and, also, with our key stakeholders?
- Who are the leaders within the sub-cultures who can best communicate wins?
- Which wins reinforce the changes in our culture and values?
- What is the appropriate reward system based on the organizations values, goals, and culture?
- What are the stories of prior organizational success, and do they still support our current program, or do they need to be replaced with new stories?
- How can we connect prior successes to the current change effort?
- Why did we have failures in the past? Have we addressed those issues to ensure they do not happen again?
- Are we building a culture that supports the behavioral traits necessary to support ongoing change, such as freedom and empowerment, in which employees are free to act within limits to meet their goals?

How do we do this?

- What are the "Top 10" items, in order, that we need to get right prior to implementation to succeed? Are these incorporated into the plan?
- How do I build short-term wins into the program plan? How do I ensure that early wins are important to key stakeholders?
- How do we track and measure wins and their impact against overall goals? How do we track early warning metrics?
- How do we reinforce and reward behaviors such as developing skills specified in skill building frameworks?
- How do we plan to communicate wins to the larger organization to sustain focus and energy?
- Who do we need to support the change effort for it to be successful? How can our program help key people meet their personal objectives?
- How will we identify short-term wins in the context of the larger program objectives?
- How will we connect wins to vision and measures to demonstrate the impact of small steps forward?
- How will we measure (objectively and subjectively) and communicate the merit of wins in relation to overall goals?
- Have we documented all processes and jobs that are changing? Are we following a structured plan to implement the process and job changes across the organization?
- Do we need to provide training to employees or customers to successfully implement change? How much training is required for each group?
- Do we continue to evaluate metrics against stated goals and reinforce success? How do we track a "Top 10" success factor list?

- How are we working with those not accomplishing stated goals to give them the confidence/comfort to take risks, build skills sets, and commit to change?
- What processes need to be enhanced to put the guiding principles into action? Who owns them? How will we implement changes?
- Do the organizational structure and governance approach support the future direction and success of the business?
- What early warning metrics can we create to let us know if we are on track before we have issues (leading indicators)? What metrics do we track daily? Weekly? Monthly?
- How do we convey required new skills using mastery frameworks that spell out detailed skills and competencies for success?
- How will the organization build a reward system that aligns with the new environment to meet multiple motivations (among people or departments)?
- Have we set goals and expectations for each individual that support the overall organization and the change effort?
- What communication processes do we put in place to provide timely feedback? How are stakeholders included in this communication process?
- Have we created evaluation and feedback processes that will be included in the plan to support new behaviors?
- Have we planned to create, communicate, and use processes to identify those not exhibiting or supporting the new strategies and behaviors and understand why this is happening?
- What are we doing to measure, communicate, and fund "learning organization" processes and activities without overbuilding the training?

Now we will revisit George as he answers the reflection questions.

What do I think/believe?

- **Do I need to change my perspective or skills to succeed? If so, what changes are necessary**

> Since all analytic efforts go through phases of discovery, model creation, refinement, validation, and implementation, I'll need to constantly adapt to be supportive during discovery phases and focused during implementation phases.

Our analytics program includes many areas of risk including new data sources, analytic tools, methods, and a culture shift. My personal risk includes a relatively recent promotion to Chief Data Officer and sponsoring the transition to an Agile delivery method. If this program is not highly successful, my job may be at risk. The organization is not very familiar with using the Agile delivery method so my choice to use this approach presents a risk to me.

Due to the number of changes and risks associated with concurrent changes, I need to continuously adapt my style to ensure success. Since all analytic efforts go through phases of discovery, model creation, refinement, validation, and implementation, I'll need to constantly adapt to be supportive during discovery phases and focused during implementation phases. While most of my career has been based on technical skills and intelligence quotient (IQ), my new challenge is to heighten my focus on emotional quotient (EQ). I need to vigilantly read all stakeholders, participants, and groups to ensure that I'm quickly and seamlessly adapting to everyone's needs. When situations and challenges arise, I'll need to ensure I don't revert to my technical skills and try to personally direct the technical resolution. It's critical that I maintain a broad, balanced perspective that encourages the entire team to own all aspects of the solution and implementation. I'll need to exercise patience since it's difficult to rush discoveries, yet stay focused to ensure implementations are rapid enough to satisfy our need for business results.

■ *How do we incorporate short-term wins into the program without impacting long-term program success, schedule, or cost?*

By moving forward with an Agile approach, we'll work in phases that allow us to naturally narrow our focus on short-term wins. At the conclusion of each phase, we'll reassess our long-term plan and validate that the next phase has the optimal scope to support short-term benefits and alignment with the vision. By incrementally increasing our analytic capability, we'll realize and record incremental business benefits. Those will continuously validate our direction and justify on-going investment. It is critical that the stakeholders align themselves with the monetized benefits. This will both ensure they can validate the success and ensure implementation in their organization.

I've also reinforced that this transformation is a journey rather than a single-thread project toward a defined outcome. I've helped the teams realize that we'll modify our plans to adapt to constant discovery and remain flexible. While our vision defines the ultimate success measures, our journey to realize that may vary and require more creativity than other initiatives.

What do I do?

■ *What decisions need to be made in the short-term to support long-term success?*

Full team engagement requires that they own all aspects of the effort. This is the antithesis of me personally directing the decisions. I will reserve a very large team room that provides ample open wall space for collaboration on white boards and flip charts. I will provide the long-term vision as an outcome and use an Ishikawa (aka fishbone) diagram to help the team brainstorm all elements that must be addressed to ensure our long-term success. We will keep this on the wall so the team can interact with and modify it.

We also keep a large Agile product backlog grid on the wall. All team members are able to understand the great ideas pending, the immediate needs about to be executed, the work in process, and recent accomplishments. By keeping it interactive and updating it daily, the team feels involved and jointly owns the outcome. This helps us generate consensus on our short-term tasks and a common understanding if one area was temporarily deferred. This improves our ability to make short-term decisions and reduce the risk of forgetting a feature that was critical to successful adoption of the analytic tools.

■ *How am I engaging key constituents to ensure their input is considered and that they are involved throughout the process in meaningful ways?*

Despite the team's high-level plan and the use of an Agile method to realize it, I've focused on extensive involvement with the executive sponsors and stakeholders. I've provided complete transparency on the overall vision and plan to achieve it. I've also made it clear that the team needs to have some flexibility to allow the data to guide their efforts. As they have feedback and guidance, I ensure that I share it with the team and discuss anything that needs to be incorporated in the development backlog.

While many meetings are an opportunity to update sponsors on our progress and educate them on the approaches, it's also vital for me to continually ask "what are we missing?" This provides an opportunity to gain their insights and ensure a stronger outcome. Many sponsors have unique perspectives that will provide additional insights or help ensure adoption of our new methods. By ensuring that I incorporate open-ended questions into every conversation with them, I've been able to balance "telling" with "listening" that benefits everybody. Their perspectives have also helped me expand my view of our enterprise.

What do we believe?

◼ *Which wins reinforce the changes in our culture and values?*

In our transition to become more analytically focused, we've put special focus on quantifying the approach and outcomes. It's important for our cultural transformation to include that aspect in our communications. We've also ensured that the venue that officially recognizes the benefits is an operational group that owns that process as part of our future state. While the initial analysis and identification may have been driven by consulting partners, the official team of record is an operational team. By reinforcing the analytic tools and processes they used, we're reinforcing the outcome as well as the process that is the basis of our future approach. By aligning it with the team, it reinforces the new processes and ensures they own the benefit realization.

If specific tools and models have been used to realize the operational "win", we've ensured other communication methods (e.g., newsletters) include more background on specifically which tools contributed and which teams helped to deliver that value. By sharing deeper credit, more teams have realized how their contributions serve the enterprise.

◼ *Why did we have failures in the past? Have we addressed those issues to ensure they do not happen again?*

We've collectively realized our past approach of using sparse data and intuition will not help us in the future. We've been careful to "attack" only that process rather than individuals or specific decisions. Since our culture honors individuals and their contribution, it could create high levels of distrust if we classified past decisions as suboptimal and associated them with specific individuals. However, our incremental gains are being celebrated with extensive communication supporting the data, tools and processes that allowed the team to be more successful. The senior leadership team is carefully monitoring the incremental results and organizational response to them to ensure the messaging is positively supporting the new methods and very delicately reinforcing how this is superior to the old methods. We've also incorporated supporting statements on how our methods will continually evolve with the next steps in the transformation.

How do we do this?

- **How do I build short-term wins into the program plan? How do I ensure that early wins are important to key stakeholders?**

   As we evaluated our development backlog and reviewed the planned availability of key analytic tools, we balanced that with the contract review calendar. We had to ensure that we wouldn't plan on utilizing tools before they were ready by selecting a review quarter that was too early. While our executive sponsors would have preferred a very early quarter, they realized we had to ramp-up the tools, processes, and organization. By allowing two to three quarters for data acquisition and tool availability, we were able to use near-term contract review sessions as part of our validation period. This also enabled us to implement solutions that had a very short delay before utilization and benefit realization. This also afforded us very early feedback for future enhancements. By maintaining a rhythm of frequent deployments, which were linked to immediate use of quantifiable benefits, our executive sponsors were able to support the results and maintain their focus on the vision.

- **Have we documented all processes and jobs that are changing? Are we following a structured plan to implement the process and job changes across the organization?**

   A key element of our Agile approach is incremental solutions building toward our vision. As part of the vision exercise, we completed an early identification of the tools, processes, and organizations that would be impacted. However, our approach requires on-going flexibility. To ensure we don't exclude any organizations, we've followed a checklist for every incremental implementation that ensures we don't miss any stakeholders. This has been easy to support with frequent retrospectives where all key stakeholders are available to ensure their organizations have been included and are prepared to operationalize the functionality.

This chapter focused on creating a program plan that spells out the actions required for successful program completion as well as the measures to ensure staying on track. The steering committee will be working closely with the program manager to support the team in meeting goals, as well as helping define corrective action when necessary. In addition to creating program plans focused entirely on the change at hand, it is important for leaders to identify areas where their own leadership skills or style may impede progress and plan developmental activities to address these. Program planning generally focuses on the changes that need to happen to systems and processes. This book expands that focus by creating a foundation for leadership development necessary to support program success. In the next chapter we will focus on communication.

We have provided blank worksheets in the appendix for you to use on your analytics program.

What do I do?

How do we do this?

CHAPTER 6
COMMUNICATE

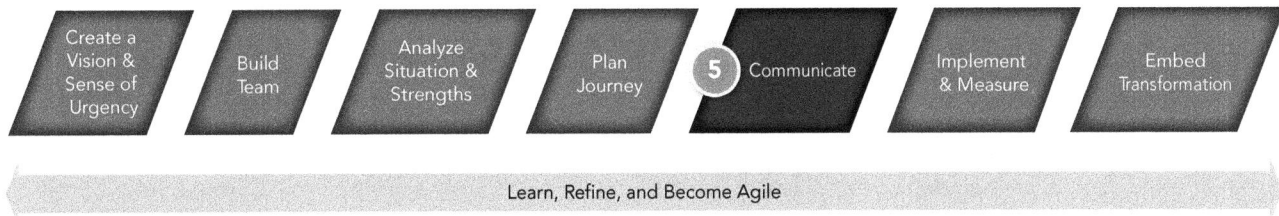

Create a Vision & Sense of Urgency | Build Team | Analyze Situation & Strengths | Plan Journey | 5 Communicate | Implement & Measure | Embed Transformation

Learn, Refine, and Become Agile

While we have a process step called communication, as a leader you started communicating as soon as you decided to turn a strategic goal into a program. When you allocated money to the program, you communicated your commitment. When you selected top talent from your organization, you were communicating through your actions. If you assigned people who were not perceived as top talent, you were also communicating.

Communication will be broken into phases based on the goal you are trying to accomplish. Initially, you want people to be aware of what is happening. Next, you want them to understand why you are making the change and why they will benefit from it. Eventually you will want them to believe in the change and take action to support it. Different audiences will be getting information at different times throughout the program. As you might imagine, the program team (those directly working on the program implementation) will need to go through communication to the acceptance process pretty quickly because you want them to accept a role on the program team. End-users of the system may not need to act until you invite them to a training class eighteen months after the program starts. You will want them to be aware that something is happening, but they should stay focused on their jobs until it is time for them to get involved. Messages and timing must be designed to help people understand and respond appropriately.

Your assessment and planning team should have evaluated the needs of multiple stakeholder groups and built a communication strategy and detailed plan summarizing audience, key messages, and vehicle used to deliver the information. This plan will then be broken into much greater detail to create an actual message map that a communication lead will manage. These messages should be time phased to address the varied timing of each audience. As an example, if you have broken the implementation into phases by location, each location will begin getting these messages based on the timing of their program launch, also known as "go live," for many programs.

> Messages and timing must be designed to help people understand and respond appropriately.

Communication supports organizational change by helping employees move up the Change Commitment Curve (see Figure 6.1) that ultimately enables them to act differently to drive

147

organizational success. The version of the curve shown in this figure is based on Daryl Connor's 1992 book, *Managing at the Speed of Change*. According to Connor, there are three specific stages in the commitment process: preparation, acceptance, and commitment. Effective communication is critical in moving people along this curve from initial information about the change to internalizing the change. There have been several variations on this curve over the years; we reference this as the foundation for change commitment discussions, because we have not seen anything more effective in discussing how people's commitment to change evolves with time and understanding.

Change Commitment Curve

Figure 6.1

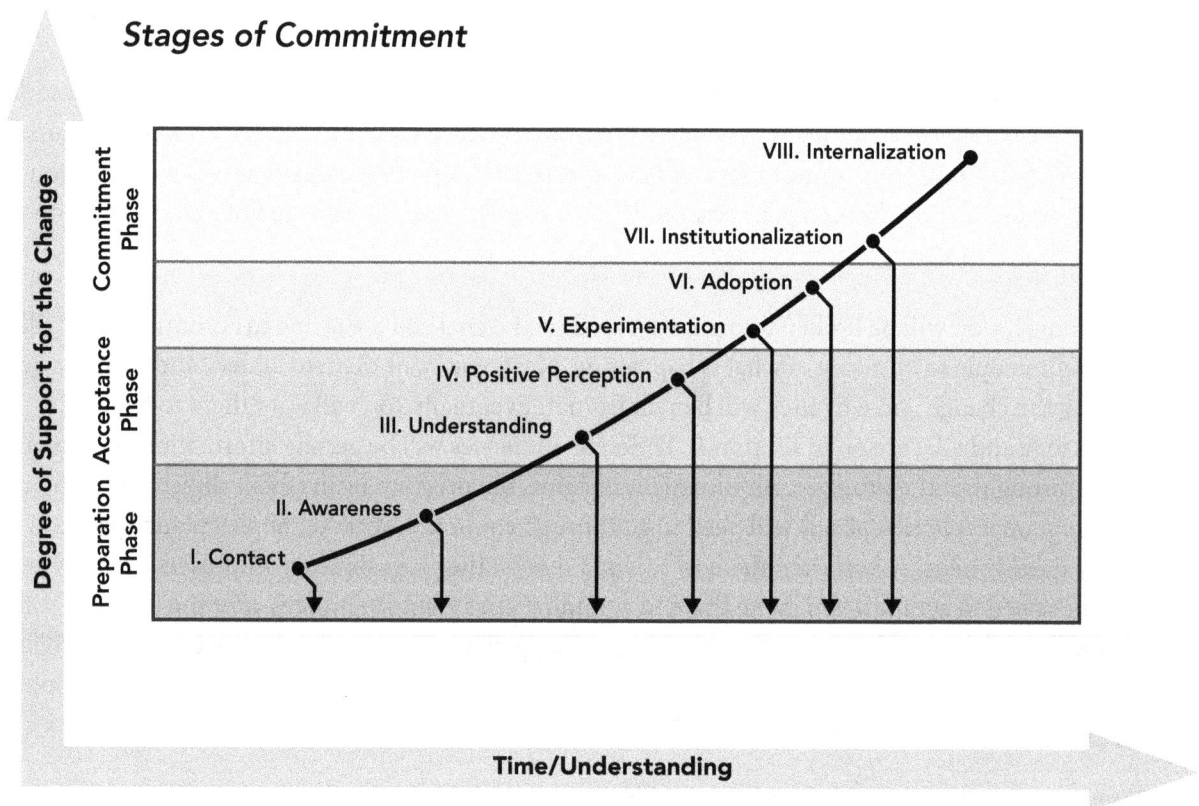

Stages of Commitment

Preparation Phase: The goal of this phase is to have successful contact with the people impacted by the change such that they become aware that a change effort is underway.

Acceptance Phase: The goal of this phase is to have those impacted by the change develop an understanding of what is involved in the change effort and believe that this change will be positive.

Commitment Phase: The goal of this phase is to experiment with the change is to allow people to test solutions and prove that they deliver value to the organization. As solutions prove effective, people can commit to a long-term integration into the organization.

Effective communication is achieved through informing, creating understanding, positive perception, and inviting participation to help achieve buy-in from individuals who will be impacted. It is important at each stage of the change commitment curve that communication is consistent, continuous, and two-way. Specific communication vehicles and messages provide impacted stakeholders with the information necessary to move along the change curve from initial contact to adoption. In addition to the written and verbal messages you send as leaders, your behavior must be consistent with what you say.

Many approaches emphasize the importance of "creating a burning platform" at this point. More research from the McKinsey study in 2009 (referenced at the beginning of the book) talks about the importance of implementing with an equal mix of positive and negative communication. We have a bias toward an approach using both positive vision and negative consequences if the vision is not successfully implemented. You will decide the right mix depending on your situation and culture.

> Effective communication is achieved through informing, creating understanding, positive perception, and inviting participation to help achieve buy-in from individuals who will be impacted.

The Communication Plan is designed to guide the program communication effort. It is generally divided into five parts:

1) **Communication strategy:** the high level description of our approach to conveying messages

2) **Detailed action plan:** indicating specifically who will communicate which messages to which groups and the expected outcome of each communication event

3) **Measurement and tracking plan:** describing how we will track communication effectiveness including sample assessments

4) **Data collection plan:** will drive our approach such as the audience analysis

5) **Templates:** for many of the communication vehicles and forms to be used in the communication process

A standard approach considers the elements of message, media, behaviors, and feedback. You will communicate clear and compelling answers to the questions that are uppermost in people's minds. You will strategically choose media to enhance the clarity and the impact of the message. Communication will come in the form of face-to-face, small group meetings, road-shows and presentations, general publications for broad circulation, and focused publications for targeted circulation. These messages will be delivered via multiple sources and forums, involving executives, organizational leaders, program team members, change network members, and others involved in the change. Over the period of the implementation, locations that have successfully implemented the change may also be involved in communicating their process for change and the successes they have accomplished.

Figure 6.2

Message

Feedback

Behaviors

Media

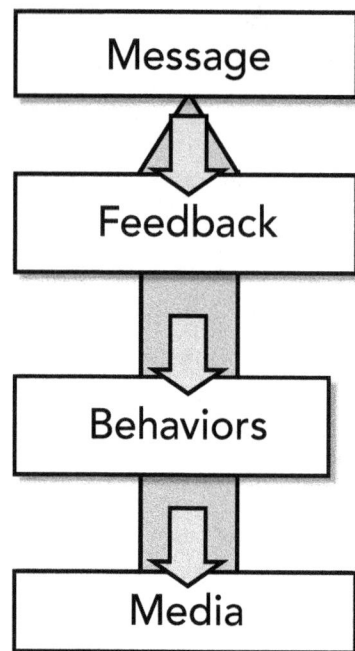

The most important factor is active involvement by executives—including the CEO for high visibility programs—and members of the program team, implementation teams, and, if you have one, the extended team or change network. Without active involvement of teams and leaders, the communication effort will be unable to achieve its objectives. Communication cannot be delegated—it is the responsibility of the leaders.

The question we get most often during change is, how much and how often do I need to communicate? It is important to remember that you convey the information every time you speak to a broad audience of people during the day. Each person may only hear the message once per month even though you are repeating it continually. According to John Kotter in his January 2007 Harvard Business Review article, "Leading Change: Why Transformation Efforts Fail," one issue with change efforts is that vision is under communicated by a factor of ten. His studies indicate, "Executives who communicate well incorporate messages into their hour-by-hour activities. In a routine discussion about a business problem, they talk about how proposed solutions fit (or don't fit) into the bigger picture."

> Communication cannot be delegated—it is the responsibility of the leaders.

Tools

George knows that ineffective communication can jeopardize an otherwise healthy and well-planned change. The following section provides examples of George's communication documents. During the assessment and planning phase, the communication lead created a communication strategy and plan. We have included some excerpts below. This approach is based on the model of cascading messages throughout the organization to build support and create a demand for the change.

Communication Objectives – The objectives of the communication effort for the program are to:

- Move everyone who needs to change along the commitment curve according to the implementation time schedule and phases

- Provide accurate information that will reduce productivity dips associated with lack of information or rumors

- Help individuals prepare for, understand, and accept changes in their jobs

- Inform and involve all impacted groups whose commitment is needed

- Enlist the help of all program team members with the communication efforts

- Build realistic expectations regarding process changes and benefits and impact

- Provide timely information, appropriately tailored for a variety of audiences

- Sustain interest and energy of program team members and implementation team members

- Maintain high visibility (mind share) with executives who face severe time constraints and maintain a high level of commitment to the program's success

- Create an image of the program as a vital component of the overall organization strategy

Critical Success Factors – The critical success factors driving this communication effort are:

- Maintain top-level commitment to the program at the executive and business unit leadership levels, especially in programs longer than twelve months

- Involve key stakeholders and executives in message delivery to ensure their genuine and on-going support

- Capture all audiences, whether directly impacted or not

- Communicate targeted relevant information in a timely manner

- Leverage process teams for communication and message development as appropriate

- Communicate consistent messages

- Ensure information is accurate

- Solicit feedback and evaluation for continuous improvement

- Ensure communication is coordinated with other change efforts and activities

- Eliminate overlap or inconsistencies across communication channels

The communication plan will contain a detailed action plan that specifies leader communication goals by program phase. We have included a sample below to illustrate what the leader communication format may be during the early phase of a transformation program.

Table 6.1

COMMUNICATION APPROACH			
Audience	**Info Exchanged**	**Vehicle**	**Frequency**
Executives			
Steering Committee	■ Analytics education ■ Status ■ Issues ■ Overall progress ■ Ongoing leadership activities and involvement	■ Analytics training sessions ■ Steering committee meetings ■ Leader/ communication discussions with change management	Bi-weekly Bi-weekly Bi-weekly
Top Executives (Direct reports to VPs)	■ Analytics education ■ What do I need to change to ensure a successful implementation? ■ Discussions of process and behavioral change? ■ Change management support ■ Coaching support ■ Impact on business strategy and the overall approach to how we do business ■ Ongoing repetition of why we are doing the program in the first place, including vision, benefits and specific progress toward realizing those benefits	■ Analytics training sessions Top executive meetings; use existing meeting structure to share program status, gain input, and begin process and behavioral changes	Bi-weekly (for local people) Use currently scheduled meetings (monthly or quarterly)
Department Managers	■ ERP education ■ What do I need to change before Day 1? ■ Discussions of process and behavioral change ■ Change management support ■ Coaching support	■ Analytics training sessions – video ■ Meetings ■ Newsflash ■ Implementation workshop	TBD TBD Bi-weekly TBD

Department Managers	▪ What impact this is having on the business in the mid-term? ▪ Resource requirements ▪ What I need to do to facilitate implementation ▪ Ongoing repetition of why we are doing the program in the first place, including benefits and specific progress toward realizing those benefits		
Staff	▪ Role of analytics in our future processes ▪ How we'll measure on-going progress ▪ Support for their roles throughout the transition	▪ Video updates from key executives ▪ Newsletter updates ▪ On-going training opportunities published on HR website	Monthly Monthly TBD

One of the tools many leaders use to communicate is ongoing talking points. Our communication lead will prepare these for us monthly, and it is our job to make sure we are communicating these points at every possible opportunity based on the communication plan and timing.

Leader Talking Points – Objective: This activity is designed to increase focus on key messages. These messages will be tailored to different audiences and will change as we move through the change process. Initially we will be focused on clarifying the vision and creating a sense of urgency, and reinforcing to the team that their contribution is valued and that they will be rewarded throughout the program with positions that take into account their new skills.

Table 6.2: Leader Talking Points Sample

MUSCLE MEMORY / THEME FOR THE MONTH

▪ **Old:** We have good people working hard. They will do the right thing, and we will be profitable

▪ **New:** We have good people working hard. By enabling them with better information that is easy to understand and advanced analytics that enable them to focus on immediate opportunities and model outcomes, they will have the information and discipline to do better things, and we will be more competitive and/or profitable

Target Audience	Questions to Ask	Messages to Convey
This Week		
Process owners and program team members	President encouraged to ask any and/or all of the following questions: ■ All VPs – What process changes are you looking at? ■ Contract review teams – How are you using quantitative measure to assess performance and recommendations?	■ I am interested in what you are doing and I would like to learn more about how you are using the new methods and the value they are adding to our business
This Month		
Program Team – communicate an understanding of their career concerns	What career concerns do your people have?	**President & VPs** We understand that while you are working on the program your peers are progressing in their functional area; we value the broader business and IT skills you are developing, and we will create opportunities for you as we progress through the program that will leverage your new skills
This Quarter		
Broad Audience ■ Location monthly discussions ■ Regional manager meetings ■ Territory manager meetings ■ Functional managers	What level of understanding do people have about the methods?	**Who:** President delivers & VPs reinforce and customize **What:** Level setting and creating a sense of urgency ■ What are business analytics ■ Business trends leveraging analytics ■ Why analytics help us address the trends

Innovative Leadership Reflection Questions

To help you develop your communication plan, it is time to further clarify your direction using reflection questions. These questions are organized to reflect the four domains introduced in Section I. As a reminder, this is an opportunity to practice Innovative Leadership by considering how your communication plan will affect changes in your intentions, actions, culture, and systems. The questions are arranged to help you explore each of these domains. The questions for "What do I think/believe?" reflect your intentions. The "What do I do?" questions reflect your actions. The

"What do we believe?" questions reflect culture. The "How do we do this?" questions reflect systems. This exercise is designed to help you practice Innovative Leadership as you create your vision and define your direction.

The table contains several questions for each domain to be applicable to a broad range of programs. We recommend you choose two to four questions from each domain that best apply to your specific situation.

Table 6.3

QUESTIONS TO GUIDE THE LEADER AND ORGANIZATION FOR COMMUNICATING TO MAINTAIN TOP LEADERSHIP LEVEL COMMITMENT

What do I think / believe?

- What do I need to communicate to others about my personal change goals? How do I solicit their input and support?
- What personal stories (actions and emotions) will convey my commitment to the change in a sincere manner and empower others to act?
- How much information do I think is appropriate to communicate?
- Am I willing to dedicate a significant amount of my time to communication?

What do I do?

- How do I show my conviction through my actions ("walking my talk")?
- How do I convey my request for input and support when I fall short of my stated goals at points along the way?
- How do I convey that although I understand others will make mistakes in the process, my expectation is that they will make a strong effort to change?
- How do I tailor and deliver messages to different segments of the organization that inclusively motivate everyone to accomplish the vision?
- How do I convey messages that will make strong statements using both the languages of feelings and of logic to appeal to multiple groups?
- How do I demonstrate humility and give credit to others?
- How do I communicate the vision in a manner that is hard hitting and realistic, yet conveys our confidence that the vision is achievable?
- How do I communicate progress, new challenges, and my support for all that is being done?
- Am I balancing communication messages to include both vision for the future and consequence if we do not change?
- How do I communicate the facts and my hopes for the future?
- How do I communicate that the balance between challenge and overload is important and that I want to maintain balance?
- How do I communicate my need and desire for accurate feedback?
- What do I communicate when situations and priorities change?

What do we believe?

- What are our beliefs about communication with regard to who does the communicating? How much information and how often do they share? Do we solicit input or just convey information?
- What is the appropriate language and message content based on the values, goals, language, and culture of each audience segment (department)?
- What type of feedback will we seek from segments to determine if they are buying into the vision (objective and subjective)?

How do we do this?

- Do we all have a good understanding of the communication strategy and our role within that strategy?
- What is our structured communication plan? Who receives communication? When? Through what channel? From whom? What are the key messages? How do we keep multiple audiences informed with the right amount of information at the right time to enhance buy-in and influence behavioral change?
- Do we have any applicable stories connected with company folklore?
- Do people understand that we need to use the rule of thumb "communicate 7 x 7 or 49" for people to internalize the messages? How do we make this expectation the norm?
- Of our current communication methods and vehicles, what will most effectively convey our messages?
- Can we combine and/or eliminate any current communications?
- Would communication be more effective if multiple programs were discussed in a joint vehicle to help the audience better understand the linkage and impact?
- How do we communicate measures and rewards for successfully accomplishing the vision (ensure a clear link between vision and rewards)?
- What communications are we currently doing that should stop because they are not consistent with our vision?
- How do we measure the impact our communication has on buy-in and change?
- How do we improve our communication based on what we learn from measurement?

What do I think/believe?

- ***What personal stories (actions and emotions) will convey my commitment to the change in a sincere manner and empower others to act?***

I'm a firm believer that actions speak louder than words. I'm sure we've all attended events where an executive kicks-off the beginning, addresses how critical it is, and then promptly leaves. Actions like that can cause team to wonder just how critical it is and about the leader's commitment. I've elected to leave more time in my schedule to attend training sessions so that I'm prepared to ask informed questions, attend town hall meetings to either insert questions or clarify major talking points, attend selected contract review sessions for more operational perspective, and actively participate in bi-weekly retrospectives. By genuinely expressing my interest and intent, team members will realize the seriousness of my commitment. I hope that my participation and my telling others about how I came to work as a CDO and how implementing this specific program is important to me because of the impact it will have on our business and our clients, will convey my commitment. I sincerely believe in this program and share not only the metrics, but my own story about why I value the work everyone is doing to make this program a success.

I've balanced that with encouraging other executives to contribute to the newsletter via interviews. By including commentary about the impact on their operations, they own their part of the vision and its realization. I've also positioned key leaders to provide video clips for internal updates. Having them provide personal stories with a few impromptu "flubs" adds a degree of authenticity to their personal messages. Most importantly, it reinforces for the entire organization that we are sharing the commitment to fulfill our vision.

■ *Am I willing to dedicate a significant amount of my time to communication?*

Absolutely! I've come to realize that communication is one of the biggest parts of being an effective leader. It's important to realize that non-verbal communication occurs when you "keep your face in the place." I'll need the support of communication experts to finalize core messages and select ideal media methods, but I can constantly communicate by focusing on the teams and the impacts on them.

I've reserved time to meet with the communications lead bi-weekly. That will give us time to review the overall progress and adjust the next steps on our communication plan. If we start receiving messages of challenges or resistance, we can adjust quickly to understand the seriousness of the concerns and either adjust the team's tasks or craft messages to alleviate the concerns.

I have learned from past programs that the reasons for resistance vary dramatically and that unhappy people can be contagious. I monitor change acceptance closely. I realize people accept change at their own pace, and they navigate the process in many different ways. I want to support this acceptance process while at the same time doing my best to ensure people are not derailing one another as they work through their own reactions to change.

What do I do?

■ *How do I tailor and deliver messages to different segments of the organization that inclusively motivate everyone to accomplish the vision?*

I have found that adjusting the message for the audience's needs requires a lot of focus. I appreciate that they will retain more of the message if I speak to their concerns and if I tell stories in addition to sharing statistics. This frequently requires planning to understand the role of the audience and some focus on their "WIFM" (What's in It For Me) by putting core messages into a context that directly impacts them (e.g., increasing customers may mean more employment opportunities, increasing profitability may mean increased bonuses, training classes will help them increase their skills and long-term success). Every level in the organization has a unique set of concerns. I've invested more time to gather those perspectives and ensure I speak to those as an outcome. I use the communication planning documents referenced earlier in this chapter to guide my initial communication. I rely heavily on a strong communication team to create these documents, and I provide ongoing feedback about what is working and what is not so they can continually update the plans.

■ *What do I communicate when situations and priorities change?*

Our use of an Agile approach and the product backlog has made this considerably easier. This also requires keeping the vision statement in close proximity so the linkage is very clear. As we complete core functionality, we have the opportunity to add more features to bolster results and acceptance. Since these are all done in support of the vision, the team has a constant reminder of the strategic alignment. Because everyone on the team understands the changes, they are also able to be informed communicators across the organization and can respond on the spot to questions.

One challenge is reinforcing that alignment message beyond the core team. We've used each successful implementation and retrospective as an opportunity to refine our plan. I've worked hard to ensure the outcomes are celebrated, and the incorporation of additional tasks is accompanied by a message that reinforces the criticality. Small changes to our short-term course have been more easily embraced. We've also reinforced that we're taking a journey and not working toward a single outcome. Embracing change throughout the transformation is a critical part of our process.

What do we believe?

■ *What are our beliefs about communication with regard to who communicates? How much information do they share? How often? Do we solicit input, or just convey information?*

In the past, the central executive or program manager was the focal point of all communications. We're changing that model with this effort. The initiative requires involvement from too many areas to have a single group address it. We've also agreed to have multiple stakeholders provide updates that incorporate some of their personal views. By personalizing the message and impact, it adds credibility for their team members.

We're encouraging completely transparent communications. We live by the mantra that "bad news doesn't age well." By getting updates published frequently, we're opening ourselves up to feedback on how we can improve. If we encounter a significant challenge, we're also open to ideas from a very large population on how to resolve it. By celebrating all successes regardless of magnitude, we're encouraging the adoption of new behaviors and practices.

We rigorously follow our communication plan at a minimum frequency. We've found it is easy to forget to communication outside of the core team (especially when they are happy with the progress). We need the periodic reminder to ensure all stakeholders share that enthusiasm and embrace the opportunity to reinforce the vision and its impact.

■ *What type of feedback will we seek from segments to determine if they are buying into the vision (objective and subjective)?*

We've positioned all leaders to participate in multiple venues to collect feedback on progress and challenges. They are very open to collecting perspectives on what is going well and what requires more focus. Through the bi-weekly retrospectives, they have ample opportunity to share how we should modify our approach to overcome concerns.

As functionality becomes available, we've reserved time for end-of-contract review sessions to understand what tools and processes worked well and what areas need improvement. This is especially critical the first few times a new method has been used. Our objective criteria will be the adoption of the tools in the analysis and recommendations. The subjective perspective will be acquired through surveys and less formal discussions. While we recognize that not all staff members will thrive with the new behaviors, we'll be open to their feedback to make adjustments to maximize everybody's potential success.

How do we do this?

◾ **Do we all have a good understanding of the communication strategy and our role within that strategy?**

During the discussions when we initiated the transformation, we discussed the significance of the communication plan due to the far reaching impact of the transformation. We collected feedback from all leadership levels of the organization to ensure we understood what they would need to know. This helped inform our communication plan and facilitated a warm reception when we presented it to the executive sponsors. Following minor modifications, they embraced it and their role in the plan. All of the listed parties agreed to their role and participation. We didn't anticipate that the executives would embrace the short video clips, but they actually seem to enjoy it the most.

While we all understand the significance, it is not the immediate nature of our leadership team to deliver this much communication. Most of our leaders have focused on execution in their specific area. It has been necessary for our communications lead to provide prompts for next steps, but those have never been received negatively.

◾ **Of our current communication methods and vehicles, what will most effectively convey our messages?**

The shortest possible answer to this question is that no single communication vehicle will deliver the message. We've had to embrace that different messages require different media. Some media foster more feedback and interaction than other channels. It's more important to mix media and be flexible based on what gains the most traction.

All past initiatives have relied on status reports and short newsletter updates. To help foster more discussion, we're opening new media channels. We've used video for the first time. This has been a mix of first-person interviews and mixed-media clips with photos and screen shots. We have found that slipping in outtakes is a popular feature. We've also embraced blogs on departmental sites. This is a great way of publishing short updates and creating open dialog through feedback. We tried a few web chats, but found them a little difficult to monitor to ensure sufficient interaction. We've also implemented town hall meetings. We've found they work better at the departmental level to ensure all participants will benefit from the question and answer period.

This chapter focused on communicating key messages according to the communication plan to move people from awareness to action and measuring to ensure you are on track. Communication involves multiple groups, and the message will be tailored to the audience and delivered through vehicles that make it easy for the recipient. As leaders, you will find that you are communicating much more than you anticipated, and yet, there will still be people who are not as aware as you would expect. It is important to communicate early and often through the entire duration of the program. In the next chapter, we will talk about moving from planning into action.

We have provided blank worksheets in the appendix for you to use on your analytics program.

What do I think/believe?

What do we believe?

How do we do this?

CHAPTER 7
IMPLEMENT AND MEASURE

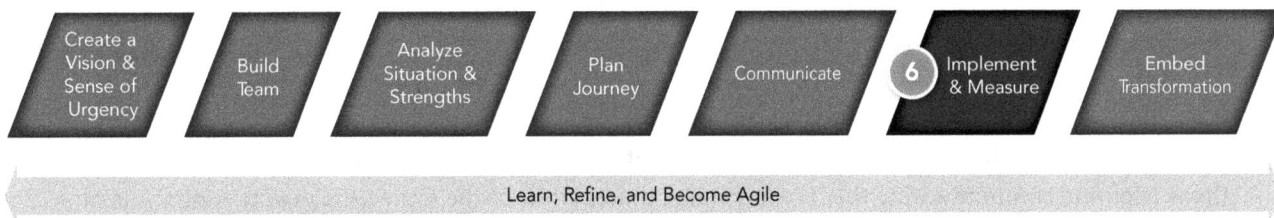

| Create a Vision & Sense of Urgency | Build Team | Analyze Situation & Strengths | Plan Journey | Communicate | 6 Implement & Measure | Embed Transformation |

Learn, Refine, and Become Agile

This chapter focuses on the implementation from a leadership perspective. The implementation of an effective analytics program requires a broad array of skills that must include technology infrastructure, database design, data integration, data quality, data science (i.e., statistics), data visualization, business process design, financial analysis, organization change management and business acumen. Additional content on those domains (and others) is available through a variety of resources. You can join the authors in those extended discussions in our LinkedIn group: Innovative Leadership for Analytics Programs.

> Your *visible* involvement is critical.

Now that you have built your team, planned your change program, and started communicating, it is time to put your plan into action and measure your progress. Your visible involvement is critical. As you have been completing the reflection questions throughout the process, the section on "what do I do" is of the utmost importance in this phase. Are you willing to be visibly engaged in the process? As you return to your plans and charters, you should have a roadmap for your role. As an example, we have included a management activity roadmap in the tools section. Depending on your role within the organization, this type of tool may apply directly to you, or you may rely on other tools such as the leader communication section of the communication strategy discussed in the prior section.

> People will listen to what you say and watch what you do.

During this phase, it is imperative that your behaviors are aligned with the change you are trying to implement. People will listen to what you say and watch what you do. Additionally, it is important that you are actively involved in communicating, monitoring progress toward implementation through metrics, and delivering appropriate positive reinforcement for success and consequences for groups that are not meeting their commitments.

While this transformation might not be the most pressing activity in your life, for the program team as they are taking action, it is often the most important professional activity in which they are engaged. Depending on the program pace, they are often exhausted, concerned about program success, engaging in new activities about which they are uncertain, and, in some cases, they experience push-

> It is important for the program to deliver results quickly to keep people engaged and committed to the vision.

back from others in the organization. The program team really benefits from a visible and supportive leader during this phase.

You have put a well-trained program manager in place to run a program. That person will use processes to review risks, issues, results, upcoming milestones, and interdependencies among other topics during the regularly scheduled steering committee meetings and also during regularly scheduled team meetings.

It is important for the program to deliver results quickly to keep people engaged and committed to the vision. You integrated early wins into your plan; it will be important to focus on delivering against those wins and communicating them to key stakeholders while at the same time maintaining focus on the long-term activities required to complete the program.

While the organization is making progress toward the change, it is also actively focused on maintaining momentum for the change effort. It is critical to keep urgency up and minimize the false sense of comfort that may come from early success. It becomes critical to remove all barriers that impede progress or allow people to continue to do business in ways that conflict with the stated change.

> Measures will show if you are on course, and also help you to learn and refine your approach where appropriate.

As the program progresses, it will be important to pay attention to morale, ensure the team is managing the stress, and staying actively engaged. If you notice challenges, it will be important to address them actively in a way that is culturally appropriate for your organization. Some organizations hold team building activities and events, and others provide additional support in the way of concierge services. One caution with team building activities: if the team sees these events as yet another activity they are compelled to do that is of little benefit during an already overburdened schedule, it will be counterproductive, and you may not accomplish your intended goal of building camaraderie.

The other key focus of this step is measuring progress. Regardless of your program, whether it is a large system change or a smaller pilot, it is important to measure your success against your program goals and also the impact you are having on the overall program goals (when possible). Some programs are structured to implement in small chunks so the impact can be measured at various intervals during implementation. Measures will show if you are on course, and also help you to learn and refine your approach where appropriate.

Tools

Most large analytics programs are managed by a project management office that develops detailed plans for time phasing of implementation. The plans will vary depending on the implementation process. If it is a Waterfall project, the changes will happen after the project is designed and built. If an Agile approach is used, small increments are deployed on a regular basis over the course of the program. As a leader, it is important to communicate your primary concerns with regard to how the implementation will begin and ensure that people are not overloaded with activities that will distract them from performing their implementation job well.

Because this transformation is being implemented using an Agile methodology, your implementation plans will take place in regular and frequent intervals (depending on the schedule you have created). This approach to implementation differs dramatically from traditional project implementations where all changes designed and developed would be implemented at the same time.

> Because this program is being implemented using an adapted Agile approach, users are seeing releases every quarter, which allows for constant course corrections based on discoveries and changing needs.

If your team is using a traditional Waterfall implementation approach, it will be important to create a month-by-month Leadership Activity Road Map to summarize leader involvement, and the communication plan specified key leader messages often using tools such as the leader talking points in the prior chapter. The roadmap will reflect the leader's monthly activities—what needs to happen month-by-month. Your role (if using this approach) is to make time to take the actions in the plans and work with the team to evaluate the impact you are making—this means things like understanding how communication impacts stakeholders. Because this program is being implemented using an adapted Agile approach, users are seeing releases every quarter, which allows for constant course corrections based on discoveries and changing needs. It is still important to clearly identify the changes and impacts prior to each release to prepare users. They need to understand who will be impacted, what they need to do differently, how it will be supported, and how the team will monitor progress. You as the leader will be highly involved in each release and your role will be tailored to the needs of the team and stakeholders as well as your personal strengths.

Your role as a leader will be to work with the program manager and others to identify gaps that others may have missed, monitor metrics, monitor risk, and provide encouragement for the team. Your program manager will provide the tools for tracking; therefore, we are not providing them in this book. For standard tools, we recommend you refer to the Project Management Institute (www.pmi.org). For more details on Agile at the enterprise level, we recommend you refer to the Scaled Agile Framework (www.scaledagileframework.com).

Stories and Examples

Now we will return to George's analytics transformation. The following Leadership Activity Road Map provides an example of the activity the leaders in George's organization will focus on throughout the transformation. The first phase followed a more prescribed path since it required coordination with the contract review cycle, and acquisition and integration of external data sources. It is important to note that as a leader you are taking action during the entire transformation initiative. Each program will have its own tailored activity road map and leader activities will vary broadly depending on the leader-specific role, culture, and program objectives. The reference to "T-" refers to "go live minus."

Table 7.1: Leadership Activity Roadmap

Vehicle	Month T-6	Month T-5	Month T-4	Month T-3
Leader Activities	• Communicate using the Program Charter as the foundation for discussions • Monitor and manage risks • Communicate that program will impact everyone in your area • Make the analytics program an agenda item on your monthly meetings • Explain the benefits associated with the initiative • Ensure contracts are completed to acquire external data	• Communicate using leader talking points • Ensure video from executive sponsors is shown at staff meetings • Monitor and manage risks • Discuss how the transition will impact your team and gather their feedback for the implementation team • Understand that your direct reports will do their jobs differently • Notify implementation team members of their role and training requirements	• Communicate using leader talking points • Monitor and manage risk • Plan work schedules to accommodate training • Explain the role employees have in the success of the program • Gather questions from employees • Approve training requirements for your analysts • Identify employees who have prerequisite training needs • Track implementation team training attendance (train the trainer) • Track pre-launch changes and measures	• Communicate using leader talking points • Monitor and manage risks • Support the need for data accuracy • Conduct change readiness assessment and take corrective action where necessary • Plan work schedules with training in mind • Approve training requirements for end-users • Plan change discussions • Understand process changes in your area • Encourage end-users to use system practice opportunities • Track pre-launch changes and measures

In addition to performing your leadership activities as noted in the Leadership Activity Roadmap (shown above across two pages), it is important to stay just as actively engaged and fulfilling your roles with the steering committee and program team as you have from the beginning of the program.

Month T-2	Month T-1	Go Live	Month T+1
▪ Communicate using leader talking points ▪ Understand your own personal behavioral changes and ensure your behavioral change is visible and supportive of the change ▪ Encourage identified end-users to attend training ▪ Use dashboard prototypes to simulate contract review session ▪ Clearly set expectations for supporting the methods ▪ Conduct job change discussions ▪ Track training completion ▪ Change integration workshops may be conducted during this time if better aligned with deployment plan ▪ Measure employee change readiness and take corrective action	▪ Conduct change discussions ▪ Track training completion ▪ Measure change readiness		▪ Track progress and reward performance ▪ Identify areas that need improvement and forward to the implementation team ▪ Identify corrective action where necessary

Innovative Leadership Reflection Questions

To help you develop your program/program plan, it is time to further clarify your direction, using reflection questions. These questions are organized to reflect the four domains introduced in Section I. As a reminder, this is an opportunity to practice Innovative Leadership by considering how your change plan will affect changes in your intentions, actions, culture, and systems. These questions are arranged to help you explore each of these domains. The questions for "What do I think/believe?" reflect your intentions. The questions "What do I do?" reflect your actions. The questions "What do we believe?" reflect culture. The questions "How do we do this?" reflect systems. Thus, we designed this exercise to help you start practicing Innovative Leadership as you create your vision and define your direction.

As a reminder, the table contains several questions for each domain to be applicable to a broad range of programs. We recommend you choose two to four questions from each domain that best apply to your specific situation.

Table 7.2

QUESTIONS TO GUIDE THE LEADER AND ORGANIZATION

What do I think / believe?

- What do I believe is an effective approach honoring the progress we have made while maintaining focus on the balance of the work that needs to be completed?

- How do I deal with uncertainty and unresolved issues and uncertainty for myself as I lead the change effort forward?

- How do I feel about getting support for my own growth and development during the implementation process?

What do I do?

- How do I publicly recognize people who accomplish wins?

- How does this communication reinforce my own values among the group?

- What changes in my behavior will demonstrate a strong statement to others and support their behavioral and performance changes as well as my own?

- What do I communicate that conveys both progress and continued urgency?

- What am I doing to demonstrate that I am "walking the talk"?

- Am I living up to the standards I have set for others?

- Am I perceived as acting with integrity with regard to meeting my commitments?

What do we believe?

- How do we monitor and build morale in different departments as they experience the pressure of balancing daily operations with change?

- What are appropriate rewards in our organization for working on programs, or picking up extra work in the department when key talent is on a program?

- How do we address situations where people or departments actively resist leadership requests to support the change?

- How do different departments (subcultures) maintain morale?

- Do we believe in coaching as to support implementation success?

How do we do this?

- What process do we use to identify barriers to success as we proceed? Do we use a change readiness assessment at multiple times during the process to evaluate changing needs?

- How do we monitor morale during the program to provide an early warning sign for potential risks? What do we do to improve morale?

- How do we minimize blocks that impaired our success in the past? Do we conduct a change history assessment?

- What have we done to identify systems that do not reinforce change and identify tools to resolve issues, such as job starts and stops and mastering new job skills?

- What processes will we establish to identify work that is no longer appropriate or necessary in the changing environment?

- What processes will we create and staff to evaluate the opportunities that can be leveraged to create additional momentum?

- Are we reviewing measures regularly and recognizing results toward the change goals?

Now it is time for George to answer the reflection questions. His answers will give insight into the challenges he has faced in past programs and what he will do this time to mitigate some of those issues.

How do I think/believe?

■ *What do I believe is an effective approach honoring the progress we have made while maintaining focus on the balance of the work that needs to be completed?*

As we continue to adopt the Agile method, it's becoming increasingly easy to value and promote the incremental accomplishments. With incremental deliveries and successes through immediate use, we're celebrating each success. It's also vital to monitor the backlog of future development needs. It can be discouraging when team members add too many new items. It has helped when they associate it with a measureable benefit.

One of the changes you will likely see is people getting more comfortable with change and liking the fact that they are not expected to get everything perfect. I have noticed that the first couple of releases are really stressful because they happen very quickly and people have not yet changed their mindset to move from traditional approach to change—that everything must be figured out in advance. The beauty of the Agile approach is that there is no such expectation of perfection but rather a shift to good enough and continual course corrections. It is fun to see people shift how they are thinking about the changes. I imagine this sort of mindset can have a significant impact on how people act in all spheres of life, becoming more comfortable with the volume of change they face.

■ *How do I deal with uncertainty and unresolved issues and uncertainty for myself as I lead the change effort forward?*

While I've embraced the Agile method we're using, I continue to recognize the analytic tools are a new area. I've realized my nature is to want to develop a foundational understanding so I can emphatically address concerns from the executive team. Unfortunately, many of the issues are beyond my areas of expertise with statistics. I've built a strong network of experts to help mitigate those areas. When necessary, I've arranged to have the appropriate experts present the solutions to ensure buy-in. I've also used extensive face-to-face meetings to proactively identify concerns and ensure upcoming presentations address them based on expert feedback and supporting examples.

As I mentioned above—the Agile method is making my discomfort with imperfect knowledge much easier because I can learn from small experiments and continue to develop my knowledge along with that of the team. These experiments take the form of releases, and we measure their effectiveness. We need to know enough to create a release that will work well; then we test and learn. I am changing my own view about how I deal with uncertainty. I am realizing through this program that there is so much to learn that I cannot stay on top of everything but I can work with our team and learn enough for the next release. I never imagined that at this point in my career I would be taking on a program that left me feeling like I do not know enough. I pride myself in being an expert in my domain. It feels both humbling and liberating at the same time. I do need to continually remind myself that I just need to have a vision of the end point but I do not need to have everything figured out right now, we will work together to get there.

What do I do?

◼ *How do I publicly recognize people who accomplish the wins?*

The most visible result of our transformation is during the contract review sessions. By ensuring the contract analysts are presenting with the new tools and methods in that forum, they are automatically receiving the credit for embracing the new approach. As they identify opportunities and support their recommendations with data, they are bolstering their own expertise and benefit recognition.

We've had our communication lead prepare video showcases that highlight specific scenarios. By showing the new graphical interfaces, having users explain the impact of the predictive analytics, and explain how it has simplified their job to prepare for a contract review, they position themselves as the owner of the accomplishment.

By quantifying the impact and explaining how it was realized, the department directors are getting the credit for helping their departments. Ultimately, by ensuring each stakeholder can claim a victory for their area, they are acknowledging the wins.

◼ *What do I communicate that conveys both progress and continued urgency?*

In my regular updates with the executive team, I provide an update on recent accomplishments. The benefits are always quantified as incremental return on the contract margin. Separately, I present a running tally of our investment and documented benefits to show the ROI. The initial investment and lagging return (due to the contract review cycle) was the most difficult part. As the returns start to build and the executive team realizes the compounding effect of the benefits, it is easy to discuss future phases and how they will deliver incremental returns. I've realized it's important to speak to both the technical and operational needs, but always with a financial perspective.

With the business units, we also tell stories of our successes. They appreciate hearing how their staff is benefiting from this effort. They have invested a lot of energy in making this possible, and stories go a long way to reinforce their wisdom in supporting the program as well as encouraging them to remain focused for the full program implementation.

What do we believe?

- ***How do we monitor and build morale in different departments as they experience the pressure of balancing daily operations with change?***

A key element of maintaining morale has been the celebration of each small win. By giving departments credit for increasing contract margins without admonishing anybody for suboptimal historical decisions, we've been able to maintain a positive outlook. The transition during implementation is the most difficult. However, since we immediately adopt the new methods that provide a significant labor savings, the teams now understand "the light at the end of the tunnel" and appreciate that it isn't a freight train coming at them.

The post-implementation retrospectives allow us to gather direct feedback from all involved teams to help us understand what would be more effective as well as acknowledge people for their novel approaches that really improved the process. While some of their feedback may be venting, it is therapeutic and acceptable. We maintain a positive outlook by asking them for a specific recommendation that will help future teams avoid some of the pain. For the times they can't make a specific recommendation, they acknowledge that it was a necessary pain. That also positions them to explain it to their peers and help them through the similar phase. By conducting these retrospectives, we can hear concerns on regular intervals and gear them toward constructive process changes, as well as allowing participants to think about what they might do differently.

Making regular time to explore concerns is important for both Agile and Waterfall implementations. I did not conduct these sessions on regular intervals until I began using the Agile methodology, and I find that it really helps build trust among team members and raise concerns to the surface rather than allowing them to stay below the surface until they are expressed in less productive and systematic ways.

- ***How do we address situations where people or departments actively resist leadership requests to support the change?***

This was a very real concern at the beginning of the transformation. We were changing decades of tradition and included one very vocal, change-resistant leader. By not removing him, we sent a message that we wanted to embrace both perspectives. However, we helped him control his messages as he received firsthand information on the positive outcomes. When his messages were strongly negative, we facilitated discussions with him to identify changes that would ensure a positive outcome. We used the results of those sessions in our action and communication plans.

Our executive team was extremely supportive and provided a strong message that "business as usual" was not going to ensure our survival. They helped establish and affirm the change imperative. Our future messages called back to that theme and addressed how the benefits we've quantified were making measurable progress to a sustainable future.

Many employees who were reluctant to embrace the transformation started to embrace it as they saw and heard about the successes each release produced. They also got to provide their input.

It seems many people just needed to see the success for themselves. Like many organizations, we had a history of "uneven" success in programs. Some ran well and created great success but others were ineffective and even disruptive. Many dedicated people became cynical, but were still dedicated and hard-working. Many in this group were just waiting to see that we were going to be one of the well-run successful programs, and then they jumped in to support us. To make this work we needed to deliver on our promises, ask for input on what was not working, and demonstrate that we made the changes they expected. It also helped that we generated results quickly and consistently. We were not saying, "Trust us—we will deliver results in a couple of years;" we were implying that we would deliver results next month. Within a few months, many of the "fence sitters" were being shifted to being supporters.

How do we do this?

■ *What have we done to identify systems that do not reinforce change and identify tools to resolve issues, such as job starts and stops and mastering new job skills?*

By adopting an incremental approach to building our future, we've easily embraced identifying change barriers. We brainstorm with the implementation team on the most effective mitigation and then assess the development impact and benefit. This has enabled the team to quantify their recommendation on when that barrier should be removed. When they've realized a permanent solution will take too long to implement, they provide more ideas to temporarily mitigate it. Overall, they've shifted their thinking from embracing a firmly defined scope and following orders to owning a solution.

It has been fun for me as their leader to see them step up with creative recommendations. My job is changing from being the one with the answers to the one who encourages them to test their ideas. I often help them refine their initial thinking, which is fun for me as their leader. I think one outcome of this program that was not built into the business case is we have identified some really strong leaders who had previously been overlooked.

■ *What processes will we establish to identify work that is no longer appropriate or necessary in the changing environment?*

As the team identifies processes or systems that require development, they are also identifying tasks that will be replaced. Since the operational teams don't have time to support both the old and new methods, they've also been very good at identifying what part of their old jobs they'll eliminate. After providing the teams with more information and methods to access it, they've very creatively identified additional savings. The biggest process we've implemented is a process of creativity to do jobs more effectively. To help us quantify the benefits of those unintended process changes, we've encouraged a "check this out" blog for individuals to showcase their new techniques. This has been a great resource to mine for unintended savings and additional success stories.

On the more quantitative side, we continue to refer back to the business case to ensure we are delivering the savings we promised when we started the program. I know it is easy to get to the end and benefit from the new tools but not rigorously enforce the elimination of work that is tradition but also becoming redundant. Leaders in each department are expected to report their approach to proactively address this and they report their results quarterly.

This chapter focused on taking action—doing the activities we defined during the planning phase. This is where much of the work is actually accomplished, and the role of the leader becomes one of staying involved in the monitoring and measuring as well as communicating, rewarding, and measuring morale. This phase of the program can last for months and in some cases years. It is important as a leader that you make sure you maintain your focus as you get pulled off to other pressing priorities. In the next chapter, we will talk about moving from action into embedding the changes systemically.

We have provided blank worksheets in the appendix for you to use on your analytics program.

What do I think/believe?

What do we believe?

How do we do this?

CHAPTER 8
EMBED TRANSFORMATION SYSTEMATICALLY

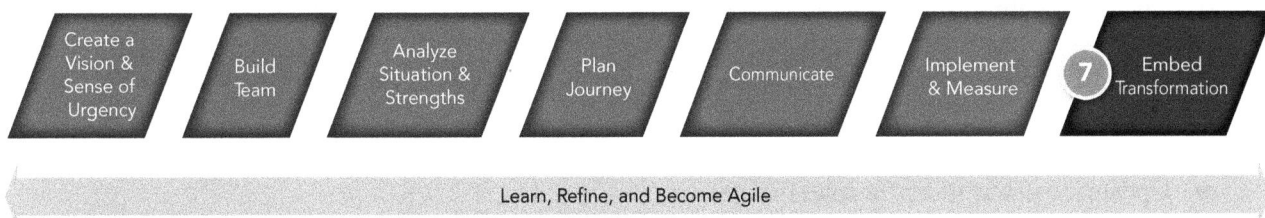

Create a Vision & Sense of Urgency → Build Team → Analyze Situation & Strengths → Plan Journey → Communicate → Implement & Measure → 7 Embed Transformation

Learn, Refine, and Become Agile

This stage is when the organization solidifies the change and it becomes part of normal life rather than a special program. Some of the actions that can encourage the change to take root include: updating the recruiting and on-boarding processes, refining the promotion process to reward those who behave in accordance with the stated goals, and creating new stories that reinforce the new culture.

To maintain momentum, it is critical to retain a sense of urgency while minimizing the sense of comfort that may stem from early success. Be aware that it is easy to stray from your goals if you declare success based on your early results, especially when other programs tug at your time and attention. One helpful shift in thinking is to see the actions you are taking as a practice. You are practicing your disciplined business activities in the same fashion that a professional athlete practices a particular sport. The most successful athletes are constantly practicing to improve, even though they may already be the best in the world. You will need to consider making time in the long term for activities that best foster success and help maintain your support system.

Therefore, ask yourself: "When I see progress, what will keep me using the disciplined practices and business processes that made me successful? How do I ensure they are sustained? I need some reminder that my progress is a result of engaged practice, and my performance is likely to suffer if I do not maintain a proper focus." These changes include both personal changes as a leader and the changes the organization is making.

Additionally, by this point, you may want to re-evaluate your goals and begin raising the bar. You will need to balance establishing a long-term discipline to sustain progress while identifying your next strategic initiatives and goals.

> To maintain momentum, it is critical to retain a sense of urgency while minimizing the sense of comfort that may stem from early success.

Tools

Below is a table you can use to capture and track processes that are impacted by the change and actions that need to take place to ensure that the overall system supports the changes. Examples of systemic changes include:

- Update new employee orientation – identify outdated content and update

- Update training – someone will inventory what training modules teach the processes that will be replaced

- Update job descriptions for roles that change

- Review/update compensation for roles that change

- Review compensation approach – is the current structure consistent with the changes we are making, and does the system incentivize the behaviors we expect?

Use the following worksheet to help you document the processes that need to be changed to fully realize the value of the programs you are completing.

Table 8.1

PROCESSES IMPACTING TRANSFORMATION BECOMING SYSTEMIC

Impacted processes	Recommended action	Expected impact	By when	Measure	Status	Process owner
Contract Profitability Analysis	1. Quantified contract profit analytics used in all contract review sessions	Deeper, quantified insight on contract profit margin	Qtr 3, Year 1	Profitability dashboard used in all review sessions	Open	Director, Contract Analysis
	2. Contract profitability projection	Increased insight on projections will lead to better profitability outcomes	Qtr 4, Year 1	All contract renewal recommendations are quantified with a multi-year projection	Open	Director, Contract Analysis
	3.					
Top 2	4.					
	5.					
	6.					
Top 3	7.					
	8.					
	9.					

Organization Transformation Reflection Questions

To help you develop your action plan, it is time to further clarify your direction, using reflection questions. These questions are organized to reflect the four domains introduced in Section I. As a reminder, this is an opportunity to practice Innovative Leadership by considering how your change plan will affect changes in your intentions, actions, culture, and systems. These questions are arranged to help you explore each of these domains. The questions for "What do I think/believe?" reflect your intentions. The questions "What do I do?" reflect your actions. The questions "What do we believe?" reflect culture. The questions "How do we do this?" reflect systems. Thus, we designed this exercise to help you start practicing Innovative Leadership as you create your vision and define your direction.

As a reminder, the table contains several questions for each domain to be applicable to a broad range of programs. We recommend you choose two to four questions from each domain that best apply to your specific situation.

Table 8.2

QUESTIONS TO GUIDE THE LEADER AND ORGANIZATION
What do I think / believe?
■ What progress have I made as a leader; as a person?
■ Am I still in the right role for my personal values and mission?
■ When I think of my mental, emotional, moral, and physical state, am I still the right person for the job ahead?
What do I do?
■ What do I do that reinforces the value of the change to individuals and to the organization?
■ What do I do to encourage people to continue the behavioral changes they made during the program?
■ How do I continue to show the new behaviors I have publicly and privately committed to?
■ How do I emphasize the focus on systematic change that encourages, but does not insist, on personal growth?
What do we believe?
■ How do we see ourselves now?
■ How will organizational goals and values change based on the change effort?
■ How do we react to old behaviors that no longer support the organization?
■ How do we shift our focus in support of long change efforts without losing the value of recent gains?
■ How do we honor our past while also making these changes?
■ How do we incorporate new jargon, best practices and human interest into emerging organizational stories?
■ How do our rewards for small accomplishments push us toward the overall organizational success?

How do we do this?

- How does the organization acknowledge people who have made the desired changes (job starts and stops) and mastered new skills?

- Do we continue to measure and reward actions necessary to sustain the change using the updated job descriptions and process metrics developed during the program?

- How does the organization fund, staff, and supply sufficient and appropriate infrastructure to support and reinforce new behaviors and culture? (These may include promotions, orientation, rewards, and recognition.)

- Have we built the changes into the ongoing training processes?

- Have we sufficiently updated employee orientation and other human resources and IT systems to support changes in goals and values?

- How have we incorporated the "Top 10 list" into our systems and processes?

- Have we reviewed objective and subjective measures regularly and recognized results that impact the change goals?

- Are we reinforcing actions that positively influence the larger vision and examining those that do not?

- Have we developed and tracked success measures and created feedback and improvement loops?

- Are we making changes based on feedback?

Now it is time for George to answer the reflection questions. His answers will give insight into the challenges he has faced in past programs and what he will do this time to mitigate some of those issues.

What do I think/believe?

- ***What progress have I made as a leader, as a person?***

Throughout this transformation, I've developed a deeper and clearer understanding of myself. I've become more aware of my weaker areas and how to bolster them through the team. I've also become more aware of my strengths and the negative outcomes if I over use them.

By remaining open to feedback from people at all levels in the organization, I've developed a deeper understanding of our operational processes and competitive pressures. I've developed more effective communication techniques by learning how to focus on the implications on the immediate audience. I've also learned the importance of refining the message based on the audience's needs.

I have started making important shift in my mindset. When I started this program I felt that I needed to have the answers and be able to see and clearly articulate the path forward. It is because of this ability that I advanced to this level in my career. I am now shifting to see my value in co-creating novel solutions to emerging challenges the company faces. During this program we certainly built on leading practices where they were available and in other instances the team pulled together, shared ideas, built on the best and rejected those that would not work. This approach worked because I had a great team who were smart and open to exploring and learning.

■ *When I think of my mental, emotional, moral, and physical state, am I still the right person for the job ahead?*

Despite periods of high anxiety and exhaustion, I've learned how to balance my life more effectively. By learning how to let the team identify risks and own the mitigation of them, I've been able to keep my anxiety levels lower. I've also learned to leverage experts (e.g., consultant deeply skilled in data mining and statistics) to mitigate the areas of high technical risk. By expanding my business acumen and honing my abilities to quantify outcomes, I'm very confident in my ability to accept even bigger challenges. I have realized the criticality of taking care of my body. I've also developed a deeper appreciation for the significance of proper nutrition and exercise to maintain a constant energy level.

I think the skills I learned during the transformation and the relationships I built with the team will position me to lead this organization for a while longer—until I am ready to take on the next big transformation (after a break from the intensity of program work).

What do I do?

■ *What do I do that reinforces the value of the change to individuals and to the organization?*

Through this transition, I've realized that sharing small wins with the people that own and execute the process is vital. They have aligned themselves with both the outcome and the process that helped them realize it. By encouraging their growth and ownership, I've been positioned for greater opportunities. While we acknowledge it will require more time to fully institutionalize the new quantitative behaviors, we have documented accomplishments and change momentum carrying us forward.

To ensure that our progress supports the organization's vision, I've consistently linked the outcomes to the financial metrics. Many status reports show steady progress toward meeting our financial goals. When the initial change rate was slower than desired, we relied more heavily on our champions to support the vision. As the profitability rates increased, we were able to communicate more proactively and let the results speak for themselves. I had to remain mindful of continuing those communications rather than assume all organization levels were monitoring the metrics.

■ *How do I emphasize the focus on systematic change that encourages, but does not insist, on personal growth?*

Throughout our transformation, we've maintained a focus on improving tools, processes, and skills to realize better business results. It is clear that not all team members are prepared for the quantitative portion of the new processes. We've been careful to respect individuals and align them with appropriate roles. It seems all teams realize that we're upgrading to a better approach, and they are actively seeking opportunities to align with that future.

While we continue to try to find roles for everyone, it has become clear that those who are willing to grow and develop are getting the most desirable roles. Their approaches solved some of our biggest challenges, and they are being rewarded. While the analytics transformation is wrapping up, the organizational transformation will continue, and it is becoming clear that those who learned and grew the most got the promotions.

We respect that some people are not motivated by growth and promotion; for those that are, we are making a clear link between growth and development and greater professional opportunities when they are available.

What do we believe?

▰ *How do we shift our focus in support of long change efforts without losing the value of recent gains?*

Through our approach of incrementally building better methods, we've helped everybody realize we'll meet our long-term goals one step at a time. One vital key is maintaining the vision statement on the wall with the supporting Ishikawa (aka fishbone) diagram. That enables us to view each step and its association to the vision. It serves as a constant reminder of all of the items we must change to ensure the realization of our vision. While the magnitude of such a list may deter many organizations, we've realized it's just a path that must be followed one step at a time.

▰ *How do we incorporate new jargon, best practices and human interest into emerging organizational stories?*

Through the use of expert consultants, we've realized the new tools are loaded with jargon and acronyms. Whenever possible, we've provided colloquial names for tools and techniques. While it helps other experts to recognize the associated jargon, it was not helping our team members. We've found it's more important for our team to embrace the processes and use of the tools than embracing all of the jargon. It's even become a source of amusement and creative outlet for our teams to name the solution phases and functions.

Beyond the use of language, we are taking away a different way of looking at how we solve problems and implement solutions. The Agile methodology has changed our thinking in some very important ways. It has impacted how we see the role of the leader and who we see as most and least effective in a team setting. It will take some time for these changes to work through the organization but at a minimum I expect the leadership team to start exploring how this transformation will impact how we run our organization in ways well beyond how we use analytics. It may go as far as refining the profile of how we hire. Should we start selecting employees for strong communication and team skills as well as technical expertise?

How do we do this?

■ *How does the organization acknowledge people who have made the desired changes (job starts and stops) and mastered new skills?*

The next generation of leaders identified themselves throughout the course of the transition. As some individuals immediately grasped the significance of the new methods and how to use the tools, their very nature and early successes garnered the support of their peers. Generally speaking, they quickly became the "go-to" person on the team for the new method. This led to natural promotions as the opportunities were available. Some existing leaders did not grasp the new methods. Through their discomfort, they took the initiative to find more comfortable opportunities. Overall, the organization found its new equilibrium.

It is important to note that with this new equilibrium, the human resources department is taking a look at their leadership development approach so that they are helping future leaders build new skills and de-emphasize those that are becoming less important. I expect them to do an overhaul of their leadership skills model in the next year. Maybe they will use an Agile approach to get input and release in stages. We would be happy to be a test case for their new thinking.

From a very high level, everybody has benefited from the new approach. Contract earnings have measurably improved, and the teams have exerted less effort to make that a reality. Due to higher earnings, the bonus pool has also increased.

■ *Have we developed and tracked success measures and created feedback and improvement loops?*

Our key processes are measurably more efficient. By measuring throughput prior to the changes and comparing to the new methods, we've been able to measure our sustainability. We've also established a culture that embraces recommendations for improvements. While the implementation team is now much smaller, they still maintain a development backlog and prioritize additional saving opportunities. A key element is to always associate each improvement with a measurable benefit. This makes it much easier to justify continued investment. It is also vital to ensure some small improvements are continuously implemented. As soon as we start ignoring the team's input, they'll stop owning improvements. Overall, the entire team realizes that the journey will continue as the final destination continues to morph.

Celebrate Your Success

What's next for you?

Throughout this book, we've provided a framework for Innovative Leadership and a process to transform your organization. We augmented the process with a series of practical questions and templates that can serve as guides. Based on our work with several hundred clients over the last five years, we offer this specific combination of tools and frameworks to guide you, the leader, and your team, to build your own Innovative Leadership and use it to transform your organization.

Additionally, we provided the story of George to illustrate how to use the transformation process. He uses the tools in the book and answers the questions to illustrate how a Strategist level leader would transform his organization. It is through George's explorations that we share the practical application of this theory with you.

Now that you have completed the guidebook for the first round, established a solid understanding of Innovative Leadership, have successfully implemented an organizational change, it is time to think about whether you want to enhance your practice and begin the process again. Do you want to build on what you have created with the Innovative Leadership Fieldbook, this guidebook, or revisit parts that may be valuable at this time? You could start from the beginning with another organizational goal, or start with yourself and examine how to further develop your leadership based on this program. Future iterations will likely take less time as you now have experience with the process. You may find that you focus in different areas based on your personal or organizational growth.

We have provided blank worksheets in the appendix for you to use on your analytics program.

What do I do?

What do I do?

What do we believe?

How do we do this?

APPENDIX
Additional Worksheets

Several of these worksheets are duplicates of what is in the chapters while others provide additional detail not included within the text. Please use them to capture your notes and work through your own program responses.

Table 1.1 – Page 34

DEVELOPMENTAL PERSPECTIVE QUICK REFERENCE

Description of Developmental Levels / Perspectives	Your Score	Your Notes
Diplomat • Demonstrates predominately concrete thinking style • Hyper-concerned with social acceptance • Emphasis on conforming to the rules and norms of the desired group • Imagines that others think and feel the same as they do		
Expert • Demonstrates basic abstract thinking • Concerned with expressing a sense of individuality in sharp contrast to others • Concerned with measuring up to the "right" standards • Can often appear to be a perfectionist • Makes constant comparisons with others to gauge identity • Can often be critical and blame-oriented • Adept at developing multiple new solutions to problems but not able to determine the best fit solution • Can begin envisioning short-term time horizons: three months to one year		

Table 1.1 Continued

Description of Developmental Levels / Perspectives	Your Score	Your Notes
Achiever ▪ Basic ability to identify shades of grey and see conceptual complexity ▪ Focuses on causes, achievement, and effectiveness ▪ Considers others while pursuing their own individual agendas and ideas ▪ Sees themselves as part of the larger group, yet separate and responsible for their own choices ▪ Appreciates mutual expression of differences ▪ Time horizon: one to five-years **Individualist** ▪ Increased capacity for advanced complex thinking ▪ Exhibits an ability to appreciate paradox in circumstances ▪ Begins to value and use rudimentary aspects of intuition ▪ Beginning awareness that perception shapes reality, including their own ▪ Self-reflective and investigative of their own personalized assumptions, as well as those of others ▪ Understands mutual interdependence with others ▪ Lives personal convictions according to internal standards ▪ Interest in feedback becomes very important ▪ Longer time horizon: five to ten years ▪ Tend to move into change agent/consultant/portfolio roles		

Table 1.1 Continued

Description of Developmental Levels / Perspectives	Your Score	Your Notes
Strategist ▪ Perceives systematic patterns and long-term trends with uncanny clarity ▪ Can easily differentiate objective versus subjective biased events ▪ Exhibits a strong focus on self-development, self-actualization, and authenticity ▪ Pursues actualizing personal convictions according to internal standards ▪ Management style is tenacious, yet humble ▪ Understands the importance of mutual interdependence with others ▪ Integrating feedback into performance is very important ▪ Tend to move into change agent/consultant/portfolio roles ▪ Well-advanced time horizon: approximately fifteen to twenty years with concern for legacy		
Magician / Alchemist ▪ Seeks transformation of organizations not according to conventional goals but according to a higher order ▪ Has a transforming ability to draw together opposites and initiate new directions from creative tension ▪ Tends to build their own novel organizations or work on their own to offer their best contribution to humanity ▪ Seen as visionary leaders ▪ May lead from behind, or in a more subtle way ▪ Time horizon: in excess of twenty years		
TOTAL:	100%	

Table 1.3 – Page 42

RESILIENCE QUICK REFERENCE

Keys to Building & Retaining Personal Resilience	Your Score	Your Notes
Manage Thinking Practice telling yourself: • Challenges are normal and healthy for any individual or organization • My current problem is a doorway to an innovative solution • I feel inspired about the opportunity to create new possibilities that did not exist before		
Maintain Physical Well-Being Are you getting enough: • Sleep • Exercise • Healthy food • Time in nature • Time to meditate and relax Are you limiting or eliminating: • Caffeine • Nicotine		

Table 1.3 Continued

Keys to Building & Retaining Personal Resilience	Your Score	Your Notes
Using Emotional Intelligence to Fulfill Life Purpose Understand what you stand for. Maintain focus. Ask: ■ What is my purpose? ■ Why is it important to me? ■ What values do I hold that will enable me to accomplish my purpose? ■ What opportunities in my professional life help me to achieve my life purpose?		
Harness the Power of Connection Practice effective communication: ■ Say things simply and clearly ■ Make communication safe by being responsive ■ Encourage people to ask questions and clarify if they do not understand your message ■ Balance advocacy for your point with inquiring about the other person's points ■ When you have a different point of view, seek to understand how and why the other person believes what they do in a non-threatening way ■ When in doubt, share information and emotions ■ Build trust by acting for the greater good		
TOTAL:		

Table 1.4 – Page 48

Transformational Leader Action-Logics Competencies At Strategist And Beyond

Competence Name	Competence Description	Score Yourself on a 1 - 5 Scale	Your Notes
Professionally humble	**Cares about getting it right ahead of being right** ▪ Committed to personal and organizational mission as "North Star" and focal point for where to invest energy in service of leaving a legacy ▪ Cares more about the organization and the result than her/ his image ▪ Freely, happily, and instinctively gives credit to others ▪ Puts principles ahead of personal gain		
Dogmatically committed to right action	**Is unstoppable and unflappable when on a mission** ▪ Has the dichotomous ability to be fully committed, hard driving, fully focused, and yet not experienced as either myopic or stubborn ▪ Has the ability to 'stay the course' when under pressure		
A 360 degree thinker	**Has the 'balcony view' of the business** ▪ Innately understand the systems, constraints, perceptions, near term, long term, and secondary impacts of business strategy and decisions, and how to transform them to complete amazing results ▪ Balances competing commitments of multiple constituents on a regular basis ▪ Thinks in terms of systems, dialogues, and transformations when focusing on constraints and perceptions—consider the organizational context when making recommendations ▪ Strong commitment to continual personal learning and building learning systems ▪ Understands cross organizational impact—striving to understand the interconnection across multiple complex systems and make highly informed decisions considering implications across broader contexts		

Table 1.4 Continued

Intellectually versatile	**Has developed interests, expertise, and curiosity beyond the job and organization** ■ Despite a devout commitment to the job and the organization, they are always interested and involved with areas beyond their comfort zones ■ Takes a special interest in political, national, and international developments ■ Use external interest to enhance legacy and provide balance in life
Highly authentic and reflective	**Is not constrained by personal appearance but is highly focused on personal behavior** ■ Highly committed to personal growth and development, and growing and developing others ■ Is so undefended and open to feedback it may be surprising ■ Seeks out discussions and feedback even in uncomfortable situations ■ Able to manage emotions in the most difficult situations—understand the impact and contagious nature of emotions so they develop skills to recognize them, manage/metabolize them, and relate to others productively ■ Able to maintain perspective in times of stress, taking a long-term view and remaining vision focused, they are less challenged by difficult situations than others ■ Demonstrates emotional courage—willing to confront challenging situations ■ Continually looking for ways to enable the organization to improve its ability to meet its mission more efficiently and effectively

Table 1.4 Continued

Able to inspire followership	**Has the special ability to connect with people at all levels of the organization to create a shared vision** ▪ Intuitively understands change, the steps to managing change, and how to help the organization overcome its resistance to change ▪ Has an innate ability to diffuse conflict without avoiding or sidestepping the source of the conflict ▪ Has a great ability to use humor effectively to put people at ease ▪ Able to relate to a broad range of people and understand their motivators and stressors ▪ Innately connect projects to the individual goals while working to overcome barriers ▪ Able to provide valuable feedback to others in a manner that is supportive of growth and development of the recipient
Innately collaborative	**Welcomes collaboration in a quest for novel solutions that serve the highest outcome for all involved** ▪ Seeks input from multiple perspectives—valuing diverse points of view ▪ Creates solutions to complex problems by creating new approaches that did not exist, pulling together constituents in novel ways, creating broader and more creative alliances ▪ Understands that in a time of extreme change, input from multiple stakeholders with diverse points of view are required

Table 2.1 – Page 57

CHANGE FOUNDATION ASSESSMENT – Key Components

Data source:	
Organizational vision:	
Strategic goals:	
Program objectives:	
Key stakeholders:	
Diagnostic activities:	
Expected changes:	
Consequences:	
Approvals:	
Program motivations:	
Implementation activities:	
Processes in scope:	
Resources:	
Risk management:	
Sponsors:	
Measurable outcomes:	

Table 2.2 – Page 59

SAMPLE PROJECT CHARTER – Key Components

1. Business problem statement:	
2. Vision and objectives	
3. Success criteria	
4. Scope	
5. Timeline and deliverables	
6. Assumptions and constraints	
7. Interconnected programs	
8. Risks	
9. Communication strategy	
10. Change management plan	
11. Team	
12. Charter approval signatures	

Table 3.1 – Page 86

TEAM SELECTION MATRIX

Criteria	Functional Expertise Y/N	Communication Y/N	Teamwork Y/N	Credibility Y/N	Trust Y/N	Culture Y/N	Commitment Y/N	Developmental Perspective (Level)	Commitment to Develop Y/N
Steering Committee									
Chair									
Member									
Member									
Member									
Sponsors									
Team Members									
Program Manager									
Team Lead									
Member									
Member									
Member									

Table 3.2 – Page 87

TEAM CHARTER

Team objectives:	
Team learning objectives:	
Major deliverables:	
Responsibilities:	
Engagement:	
Timing:	
Measure of success:	
Resource requirements:	

Table 4.3 – Page 110

STAKEHOLDER IMPACT ANALYSIS

Stakeholder name (Group)	Who to interview	Impact of change	Perception of change	Role supporting change	Level of commitment (h, m, l)

Table 4.4 – Page 111

USER IMPACT ANALYSIS

Function / process	Process / people changes	New skills	Position changes

Table 4.5 – Page 112

CHANGE INITIATIVE INVENTORY

Change initiative	Description	Who impacted (user groups / plants)	How does it impact other initiatives?	Timing

Table 5.2 – Page 132

LEADER DEVELOPMENT WORKSHEET – Evaluate and Select Behavioral Change Priorities

Key Actions	Detailed Action Planning	Skill 1	Skill 2
Select Behaviors	Which behaviors do I want to improve or change? Which behaviors do I perform well that I would like to enhance?		
What are the consequences of this behavior?	What will happen if I continue to demonstrate this behavior in the future? How does this behavior impact my customers? How does it impact my career? How are my colleagues impacted? How is my organization impacted?		
Why do I demonstrate this behavior?	I have developed behaviors over the course of my life because they make sense. What has changed that now makes this behavior ineffective?		
How would I like to perform in the future?	Write an end-result statement describing the changes I will make and the impact of those changes. What will an observer see when I have made this change?		
Who will help me change?	Who could I ask to provide me with feedback on how I am doing? Who would be a good mentor?		
What type of support do I want?	Make an agreement with a person you trust about how you would like to support one another in changing behaviors. How will that person hold me accountable for taking this step? How will I support them in changing their behavior? Is there a group that will support me long term?		
What will I do or not do?	What other actions could I take? What am I willing to commit to doing? What am I committed to stopping?		
When will I complete actions?	When will I have completed action items?		

Table 5.3 – Page 133

DEVELOPMENT PLANNING WORKSHEET

Current State	Future State / Goal	Actions	By When?	Measure - How do you know?

Table 8.1 – Page 182

PROCESSES IMPACTING TRANSFORMATION BECOMING SYSTEMIC

Impacted processes	Recommended action	Expected impact	By when	Measure	Status	Process owner
Top 1	1.					
	2.					
	3.					
Top 2	4.					
	5.					
	6.					
Top 3	7.					
	8.					
	9.					

Resources

This section includes additional recommendations to augment the fieldbook for those who want more in-depth information.

Resources Chapter 1

One of the most powerful tools for understanding ourselves is the Enneagram, an ancient symbol of unity and diversity, change and transformation. There are several very solid enneagram resources. The one we use most often for leadership groups is: www.enneagraminstitute.com

www.enneagraminstitute.com

The theoretical research of Susann Cook-Greuter and Terri O'Fallon provide the most recent and complete references available in support of Developmental levels and their applications. Both can be found on their websites.

www.cook-greuter.com
www.pacificintegral.com

Cindy Wigglesworth provides a spiritual intelligence competency model designed to improve leadership effectiveness.

www.deepchange.com

Ken Wilber is the original philosopher and founder of Integral Theory. He has written over 30 books on the subject. He founded the Integral Institute whose mission is: to awaken humanity to full self-awareness. By providing research, education and events that foster intentional, behavioral, cultural and social self-awareness, the Institute helps global leaders from all arenas to improve the human condition. The Institute's vision is that humanity lives with the awareness necessary to compassionately integrate the fragmented and partial perspectives of differing pursuits of the good life.

The Institute aims to help solve the world's most complex problems. Among the primary goals of the Institute are research and cultivation of leadership of complex, global issues facing humanity in the 21st century, and in particular, those issues that can only be solved with a comprehensive, Integral and non-partial approach to the complex interdependencies that tend to characterize these issues. Global warming; evolutionary forms of capitalism; and the culture wars in political, religious, and scientific domains are all examples of problems to which the Institute hopes to bring new clarity.

www.integralinstitute.org

References

Berez, Steve Phillips, Stephen and Ramirez, Jean-Claude, "Five Keys to IT Program Success." *Bain Industry Brief,* June 2012.

Brown, Barrett. "Conscious Leadership for Sustainability: How Leaders with Late-Stage Action Logic Design and Engage in Sustainability Initiatives." Ph.D. diss., Fielding Graduate University, 2011.

Bylund, Anders. "How Will the Internet Of Things Help GE?" *The Motley Fool,* June 2014.

Collins, Jim. *Good to Great: Why Some Companies Make the Leap... and Others Don't.* New York: HarperCollins, 2001.

Cook-Greuter, Susanne. "A Detailed Description of Nine Action Logics in the Leadership Development Framework Adapted from Leadership Development Theory." www.cook-greuter.com. 2002 website accessed 5/25/14.

Csikszentihalyi, Mihaly. *Flow: The Psychology of Optimal Experience.* New York: Harper Perennial, 1990.

Favaro, Ken. "Big Data Strategy: s+b's Strategy of the Year." *Strategy and Business,* January 2014.

Fitch, Geoff, Venita Ramirez, and Terri O'Fallon. "Enacting Containers for Integral Transformative Development." Presentation: Integral Theory Conference, July 2010.

Gauthier, Alain. "Developing Generative Change Leaders Across Sectors: An Exploration of Integral Approaches." *Integral Leadership Review,* June 2008.

Goleman, Daniel. *Emotional Intelligence.* New York: Bantam Books, 1995.

Goleman, Daniel, Richard E. Boyatzis, and Annie McKee. *Primal Leadership: Learning to Lead with Emotional Intelligence.* Boston: Harvard Business School, 2002.

Goleman, Daniel. *Working with Emotional Intelligence.* New York: Bantam, 1998.

Heath, Chip and Dan Heath. *Switch: How to Change Things When Change Is Hard.* New York: Broadway, 2010.

Heifetz, Ronald A. and Laurie, Donald A.. "The Work of Leadership." *Harvard Business Review on Breakthrough Leadership.* December 2001.

Heifetz, Ronald A., Alexander Grashow and Marty Linsky. *The Practice of Adaptive Leadership: Tools and Tactics for Changing Your Organization and the World.* Cambridge Leadership Associates, 2009.

Howe-Murphy, Roxanne. *Deep Coaching: Using the Enneagram as a Catalyst for Profound Change.* El Granada: Enneagram, 2007.

Isern, Joseph, Mary C. Meaney and Sarah Wilson. "Corporate Transformation under Pressure." McKinsey & Company, 2009.

Klatt, Maryanna, Janet Buckworth and William B. Malarkey. "Effects of Low-Dose Mindfulness-Based Stress Reduction (MBSR-ld) on Working Adults." Health Education and Behavior. Vol. 36, no. 3. 2009: 601-614.

Kleyman, Bill. "The Big Data Battleground: Analyzing the Big Picture." *Data Source Knowledge*, September 2012.

Kotter, John P. "Accelerate!" *Harvard Business Review*, November 2012.

Loehr, Jim and Tony Schwartz. "The Power of Full Engagement: Managing Energy, Not Time, Is the Key to High Performance and Personal Renewal." Free Press Publications.

Loehr, Jim and Tony Schwartz. "The Making of a Corporate Athlete." *Harvard Business Review*. 2001.

Maddi, Salvatore R. and Deborah M. Khoshaba. *Resilience at Work: How to Succeed No Matter What Life Throws at You*. New York: MJF, 2005.

May, Thornton. *The New Know: Innovation Powered by Analytics*. New Jersey: John Wiley & Son, Inc,. 2009.

May, Thornton. "The Path to Big Data Mastery." *Computer World*, February 2014.

May, Thornton. "Reflections on inflections." *Computer World*, March 2014.

May, Thornton. "Renaissance Lessons for Modern CIOs." *Computer World*, May 2014.

Metcalf, Maureen. "Level 5 Leadership: Leadership that Transforms Organizations and Creates Sustainable Results." *Integral Leadership Review*. March 2008.

Metcalf, Maureen, John Forman, and Dena Paluck. "Implementing Sustainable Transformation – Theory and Application." *Integral Leadership Review*. June 2008.

Metcalf, Maureen and Paluck, Dena. "The Story of Jill–How an Individual Leader Developed into a 'Level 5' Leader." *Integral Leadership Review*. June 2010.

Northouse, Peter G. *Leadership: Theory and Practice*. Thousand Oaks: Sage Publications, 2010.

O'Fallon, Terri, Venita Ramirez, Jesse McKay, and Kari Mays. "Collective Individualism: Experiments in Second Tier Community." Presented August 2008 at the Integral Theory Conference.

O'Fallon, Terri. "The Collapse of the Wilber-Combs Matrix: The Interpenetration of the State and Structure Stages." Presented July 2010 at the Integral Theory Conference (1st place winner).

O'Fallon, Terri. "Integral Leadership Development: Overview of Our Leadership Development Approach." www.pacificintegral.com, 2011.

Press, Gil. "IDC: Top 10 Technology Predictions for 2014." *Forbes*, December 2013.

Richmer, Hilke R. An Analysis of the Effects of Enneagram-Based Leader Development On Self-Awareness: A Case Study At A Midwest Utility Company. Ph.D. diss., Spalding University, 2011.

Riso, Don Richard, and Russ Hudson. "The Wisdom of the Enneagram." *The Complete Guide to Psychological and Spiritual Growth for the Nine Personality Types*. New York: Bantam, 1999.

Riso, Don Richard, and Russ Hudson. *Personality Types: Using the Enneagram for Self-Discovery*. New York: Houghton Mifflin, 1996.

Rooke, David and William R. Torbert. "Organizational Transformation as a Function of CEOs' Developmental Stage." *Organization Development Journal* 16 (1): 11-28 (1998).

Rooke, David and William R. Torbert. "Seven Transformations of Leadership, Leaders are made, not born, and how they develop is critical for organizational change," *Harvard Business Review,* April 2005.

Suh, Inhi Cho. Vice President of Big Data, IBM, "Five Ways Companies Can Compete Using Big Data and Analytics." *Forbes*, April 2014.

Terrell, Steve. Learn From Experience. *Leadership Excellence*, June 2013.

Terrell, Steve. Learning Mindset: Developing Leaders Through Experience. trainingmag.com. March 2014.

Terrell, Steve, and Katherine, Rosenbusch. "How Global Leaders Develop," *Journal of Management Development* 32 (10): 1056-1079 (2013).

About the Author

Maureen Metcalf

Maureen Metcalf is the Founder and CEO of Metcalf & Associates, Inc., a management consulting and coaching firm dedicated to helping leaders, their management teams and organizations implement the innovative leadership practices necessary to thrive in a rapidly changing environment.

Maureen is an acclaimed thought leader who developed, tested, and implemented emerging models that dramatically improve leaders and organizations success in changing times. She works with leaders to develop innovative leadership capacity and with organizations to further develop innovative leadership qualities. Maureen is on the forefront of helping organizations to explore these emerging solutions for long term organizational sustainability.

As a senior manager with two "Big Four" Management consulting firms for 12 years, Maureen managed and contributed to the successful completion of a wide array of projects from strategy development and organizational design for start-up companies to large system change for well-established organizations. She has worked with a number of Fortune 100 clients delivering a wide range of significant business results such as: increased profitability, cycle time reduction, increased employee engagement and effectiveness, and improved quality.

James Brenza

James is the Chief Data Officer for InXite Health Systems. He is also Vice President, Data and Analytics Practice for Pillar Technology. He provides over 20 years of technology leadership to drive the use of data and analytics for sustainable competitive advantage. His background includes analytics leadership, business process reengineering, program management and software development. He has a broad delivery background in industries including finance, manufacturing, pharmaceutical, retail and higher education. He is a published author focusing on leading business transformation through analytics. James is also active in the Columbus start-up community as an advisory board member and Chief Data Officer.

In prior roles, he was the Chief Data Officer for The Ohio Sate University and a managing consultant for IBM. He has also held technology leadership roles for Kroger, GE and BMW Financial.

When he occasionally pulls his nose out of books, he does some amazing woodworking.